blue
rider
press

RULES
FOR OTHERS
TO LIVE BY

ALSO BY RICHARD GREENBERG

RULES

FOR OTHERS

TO LIVE BY

Comments and
Self-Contradictions

Richard
Greenberg

BLUE RIDER PRESS

NEW YORK

blue
rider
press

An imprint of Penguin Random House LLC
375 Hudson Street
New York, New York 10014

Copyright © 2016 by Richard Greenberg
Penguin supports copyright. Copyright fuels creativity, encourages diverse
voices, promotes free speech, and creates a vibrant culture. Thank you for buying
an authorized edition of this book and for complying with copyright laws by
not reproducing, scanning, or distributing any part of it in any form without
permission. You are supporting writers and allowing Penguin to
continue to publish books for every reader.

Blue Rider Press is a registered trademark and its colophon is
a trademark of Penguin Random House LLC

Library of Congress Cataloging-in-Publication Data

Names: Greenberg, Richard, author.
Title: Rules for others to live by : comments and self-contradictions /
Richard Greenberg.
Description: New York : Blue Rider Press, 2016.
Identifiers: LCCN 2016016446 | ISBN 9780399576522 (hardback)
Subjects:
LCSH: Greenberg, Richard—Humor. | Dramatists,
American—20th century—Biography. | Conduct of life—Humor.
BISAC: HUMOR / Form / Essays. | BIOGRAPHY & AUTOBIOGRAPHY /
Editors, Journalists,
Publishers. | HUMOR / General.
Classification: LCC PS3557.R3789 Z46 2016 | DDC 812/.54 [B]—dc23
LC record available at https://lccn.loc.gov/2016016446
p.   cm.

Printed in the United States of America
1   3   5   7   9   10   8   6   4   2

Book design by Amanda Dewey

Penguin is committed to publishing works of quality and integrity. In that
spirit, we are proud to offer this book to our readers; however, the story,
the experiences, and the words are the author's alone.

For Shirley Levine Greenberg,
who admired writers

Contents

CITY FRIENDS

STORYTELLING

THINGS ARE LOOKING UP, MAYBE; AND BACK

Apology to Oprah

Everything in this book is true.

Some names have been changed.

A few names, though the real names, have been misspelled.

Some of the events described, while they actually happened, did not actually happen in the rooms in which I've placed them.

If you think a character is based on you, and you do not like that character, that character is not based on you.

A few of the people I describe do not, in the strictest sense of the word, exist.

One or two of the stories that feature people who do not exist may not have happened.

The character called "I" is a total fabrication.

This book is a work of fiction.

Introduction

The young woman—a girl, really: eighteen—was touching. She was writing plays and frustrated that they were invariably about herself.

I failed her. My advice boiled down to "There, there." She was young; later she would be old. Things would sort themselves out.

On the ride home from her question, I gave myself a do-over. Make a helpful answer. In the mirage of a second draft I said this:

"Acknowledge that you're the center of the universe, then radiate."

She wanted a specific exercise; she wanted *out*!

Go online, I told her, and bring up the front page of the *New York Times* from the day you were born. Read every article. In amazement.

True, we no longer believe that A caused B then C happened, as playwrights who thought they were emulating Ibsen did. This should not be taken to mean that nothing causes anything. More that everything causes everything. We travel through clouds of influence. The *New York Times* will show you some of the influences into which you were born.

Do they stun you? Does any of it seem familiar? The *New York Times* was already guessing what would be happening now; was it naive? Does anything explain that thing your dad is always saying? Does some fact interest you for reasons that apparently have nothing to do with you? Pursue it. In some distant manner, it's connected to you.

The best thinking says "the self" is a fiction (I have a piece about that), yet it's a fiction that we all believe, our most intimate experience. Maybe it's nothing more than our tendency to repeat. Maybe we repeat because when we do, we recognize the behavior and the familiarity is comforting. So that the self is just the consolation of our tendencies. This is too deep for me.

The reason I never write personal essays is that I have no idea who "I" is. Setting out to write some, I had to locate my main tendencies and, for the sake of convenience, label them.

I would say I am an Urban Recluse.

The phrase is problematic, luckily. My brother, who trained as an economist, once accused me, as though I transgressed, of being the kind of human integer that screwed up his quantitative analyses (at last, a virtue!). Maybe so. My life goes heavy on the interiors; still, it's crucial that their windows look out on the densest, most complex, most confounding system of social arrangements yet devised. It's what I like to watch. Then I make up stories about it.

My tendency.

When I call myself an Urban Recluse, I know the phrase doesn't constitute an identity, much less a self. It's the angle from which I radiate, and that's all I have to say about it.

[**MANIFESTO**]

Wisdom

I am a very wise man.

How I know this is, a number of people have told me so, among them several who consider my intelligence average and my talent meh. Wisdom is another quality altogether.

It might surprise you to learn of my wisdom, especially given that my life is patently disastrous. It's the old saw about doing and teaching, which, in addition to being a truism, is true. You can see it in all kinds of situations. For example, drawing from my own world, there's not a theater critic alive capable of writing a play, yet two of them are competent reviewers.

When it comes to developing wisdom, failure turns out to be an advantage. I once talked to a group of playwriting students among whom, startlingly, was a woman who had written four novels that had been decent commercial and strong critical successes but who claimed she had no idea what she was doing. I didn't believe this. You simply cannot have four consecutive flukes. She was adamant. Years later,

I read a book about the early days of Barbra Streisand and I understood what the novelist meant.

It seems that Barbra never valued her singing because it was too easy for her. "I just open my mouth and it comes out right," she said.

This is what the novelist found so perplexing: she had stories to tell and she knew how to tell them. Having read novels, she was able to write novels. She knew what she was *doing*; what she didn't know was how to *describe* what she was doing.

I don't teach playwriting very often, but when I do I'm pretty good at it because I've faltered as a playwright in so many ways. I look at the student plays and think, almost dotingly, "Ah yes: that mistake! Remember it well. Made it myself in the hardscrabble winter of 'eighty-six." Failure begets consciousness begets, sometimes, technique.

I've messed up at living even more spectacularly than I have at writing, thus my status as a fount.

If I have a limitation as a wisdom-giver, it's my too-easy assumption that others are far more capable than I am. As a result, I become testy when they don't follow the rules I set out for them, rules I would never think of applying to my own life. I'm trying to get better about this.

Before I was a wise man, I believe I was a bit of a charlatan. That was during my late twenties and early thirties. People were always coming up to me and thanking me for changing their lives when I said to them such-and-such. The problem was that when they quoted such-and-such back to me, I neither remembered saying it nor had any idea if I believed it. In those days, my wisdom was what I would call cadential wisdom. The sentences I put out had the shape and rhythm of truth but were actually rather vapid. You can go far on this talent.

The late Maya Angelou wrote the beautiful memoir *I Know Why the Caged Bird Sings*. After that, she became a public figure, in which role she was a virtuosa of cadential wisdom, and the power of the curious things she said was magnified by her extraordinary speaking voice. This is why when Oprah shares something like "Dr. Angelou once said to me, 'Oprah, it's cold out; put on a sweater,'" it never quite hits *us* with the prophetic force with which it evidently bushwhacked Oprah.

Elaine Stritch, rest in peace, was a great actress, much-loved woman, and riveting Broadway star. She was also imputed with a high degree of cadential wisdom. Show folk thought she carried all sorts of salty insight. I worked with Elaine for two weeks in the late nineties and I thought she was out of her mind. Being out of your mind is not a detriment when it comes to cadential wisdom, as long as you find adherents for your particular wisdom-giving style. This sort of thing has been going on forever. In its modern form, it can be traced back to the sixties, when, traditional authority having been lain siege, people were freed up to submit to whatever bogus, mumbo-jumboing authority they found sexy. It made no difference that the things these authorities preached never tallied with what was really going on, because so many people had stopped thinking. They had simply stopped thinking.

$$\begin{bmatrix} \text{CITY} \end{bmatrix}$$

Selves

I used to have a wildly exaggerated reputation for being a hermit.

I still have the reputation, but it's no longer so exaggerated.

When you spend much of your time inside, it sharpens your sensitivity to what goes on when you're outside, in the public spaces.

For example, yesterday morning, in the course of a single block, I noticed four extraordinarily handsome men. Everyone else ignored them.

From time to time, you'll see an extraordinarily handsome man who turns out to be a porn star and you'll wonder, "Why porn when he could be making a fortune on the runways of Milan?"

Well, here was my answer: He could not be making a fortune on the runways of Milan. Handsome men are not at a premium. You can get them by the blockload on Ninth Avenue.

If I went out more often, my sensibilities would have been too coarsened for me to figure this out.

People who plunge through Midtown every day develop techniques for getting through. Selective deafness. Visual blurring. A kind of ghostlike permeability. They are not there, they are between theres, because actually to be there is literally intolerable.

I find myself in Midtown occasionally and am never out of it before I've resolved to retire to the foothills of Vermont and open a store that sells dry goods and tea. For though I can avail myself of the methods of the daily travelers, I can only do so with partial success. Unlike them, I can be got at.

This is where it would be helpful to have the skills of a good racist.

Racism, historically, has been both a psychosis and a labor rationale, but more pervasively, I think, it's been a convenience.

There is simply too much assaulting us, more to care about than we can possibly cope with. How better to deal with this than to lop off whole populations from the arena of human concern? The broad stroke: efficient.

And this is what the daily traveler does. The blurring and the deafening feel like self-abnegation but, in truth, they annihilate others, turning persons into extras, not really there though sometimes smelly.

Once in a while, however, and without warning, the unbearable thing happens: the extras become selves.

Now neuroscientists will tell you that if you trace the concept of the "self" down to its root, you will discover there is no such entity. They are undoubtedly right about this, and the hell with them.

For my purposes, the self is that being that emerges at four o'clock in the morning when you wake with a stuffed nose, gasping for air, and you can't get enough air no matter what you do, and though you don't believe in God you do believe in damnation and that whatever sorting office arranges eventualities has you marked for this eternity of gasping, and while eternity is palpable, something you can feel intimately, the mercy of oblivion is beyond comprehension.

So to be making your way through the human glut that is Times Square at any hour and to pause at a Don't Walk sign and suddenly be gripped by the awareness that you're surrounded by selves—your fellow damned—is horrific. It's like a fever breaking or a fever cresting. You go cold and your forehead dampens and there's a sensation of changing altitudes even though you're standing in place. You ache to have your tools back, your sad, sorry, broken ones, to blur, to deafen, to annihilate. But it's only once you've gotten back home—door locked, shoes off, drink in hand—that any degree of calm can be restored. And it's a cold calm.

There's a quieter version of this inimical awareness, and in some ways it's even more disturbing.

It comes when you turn on the local news and find yourself watching a wafer of a man, handcuffed and being escorted by police out of the basement apartment in Queens where he has just hacked to death his sweet wife and four small children.

Then there's a close-up.

And you recognize him as the delivery guy from your Chinese restaurant.

Only you're a racist so, actually, you *mistake* him for the delivery guy from your Chinese restaurant.

Well, You've Just Been a Delight,
or
New York City in the Eighties

In the eighties in New York City, there was a thriving phenomenon known as public access cable TV.

For what I suppose was a nominal fee, any member of the citizenry could purchase airtime and put on a show.

The programming tended to have certain features in common, among them smeary lighting, chaotic structure, and more or less pornographic content.

One night, a nice, motherly lady was interviewing a handsome young man.

She had a strong midwestern accent and wore that hairdo that was favored at the time by a cross-demographic of middle-aged suburban housewives and militant lesbians: shorn at the sides with a lot of spiky volume on top and arrowheads next to each ear. For some reason she reminded me of Betty White.

Her guest was well built and rangy and a little goofy in an East Village way. He was the sort of guy who made money cleaning Keith Haring's paintbrushes.

The nice Betty White lady had chosen to interview him for two reasons.

1. He had AIDS.
2. He liked having sex with dogs.

Especially the latter—she couldn't get enough of his shagging dog stories. A little shyly, she admitted that when she first came to New York years and years and years before, one of the things that fascinated her was the prospect of sex with a collie. Once she had been at a party where someone passed around snapshots depicting such an act and she said (here she mimed holding the photos at arm's length), "Oh yes, very interesting," but, alas, her ambition was never to be realized within the privacy of bedroom or kennel.

"How do you go about such a thing?" she asked with wonder. "How do you make it happen?"

So Keith Haring's assistant launched into a description of his techniques of wooing. And make no mistake about it—there *was* wooing involved, because he was a stand-up guy and the sex he had with dogs was strictly consensual.

You started by scratching the dog behind his ear.

There wasn't much time for AIDS, what with all the dog-fucking to talk about, and they never got around to the question that interested me most, which was is it possible to give a dog AIDS or do you wear a condom when you fuck a dog or what?

He did allow that he found having AIDS "a really interesting experience."

At that point their time was up and she put a hand on his knee and, with her nicest Betty White smile, said,

"Well, you've just been a delight."

Mediocrity: An Appreciation

The neighborhood around me—and by "neighborhood," I suspect, is denoted only several blocks—is protected by the Landmarks Commission, I've been told, though few of its buildings have received landmark designation.

What's being preserved then is a definable essence—a matter of scale, materials, and, perhaps less definably, style.

As a result, when new buildings have gone up, they haven't been blockbusters. They're sometimes inaesthetic and often of no social value, but perforce—per law—they fit in.

There's a new building across the street from me, in plain view out my window. It's made up of condominiums for the wealthy and a few boutique stores, and it replaced a building that for half a century served as public housing.

I will say here and now that that is a very terrible thing and, so saying, will register myself as one of the good guys, then go mum on the subject. Because though I could work up a searing diatribe, and mean it, it would be both deeply familiar and utterly ineffectual. We all know how the city is drifting and we all know that the drift is, by and large, unspeakable.

I will say a word about the building that was torn down.

It had a single quality to recommend it, and that only to extreme historicists: it smacked of the year it was built, 1960. In 1959, it would have been avant-garde; by 1961, passé.

It was five stories high, of adobe-tinged brick on the top floors and broken tiles below. There were columns on the ground level so that the entries were set back, establishing a dark walkway excellent for muggings. The graffiti was not of Basquiat quality and once sprayed on was never erased.

Public housing has two main functions: to meet a need and to punish the needy for having that need. In addition, it must never inspire resentment among those who get their shelter full price.

To those ends, the windows of this building were minuscule and there weren't enough of them; the hallways were fashioned from the materials of rebuke; and the lighting, intermittent, was of the unmediated fluorescent kind that saps vitamins.

I suppose, in its discouraging way, it functioned well enough over its half century of existence. At least, I'm not aware of any legends touting its infamy.

Obviously, I haven't a clue what's happened to its last tenants.

Nor have I met any owners of the new apartments.

Really, I'm writing about an exchange of buildings only.

As a physical entity, the new structure is a vast improvement in every way, while remaining committedly mediocre.

Mediocrity is no bad thing.

Subject to the landmark regulations, this replacement building, though capacious, is modestly scaled. It stands at the corner of a row of beautiful old red-brick townhouses and is itself made of red brick in a shade that blends. To attract buyers, it's had, in a quiet way, to declare its modernity, and, on the exterior at least, it has done this mostly through fenestration. As though in rebuttal to its predecessor's porthole-like stinginess, this new place resounds with windows—large, open, picture windows, and tall, narrow, mullioned windows—and the windows are arranged craftily to convey a light sense of energy, invigorating but not hectic. Relatively few people will live in the apartments, more will shop in the small stores, but mostly what will happen to this building is people will walk past it, and its windows and string courses have been thoughtfully designed to encourage a pedestrian's step.

What makes the building mediocre is that it doesn't have an original thought in its head. You see nothing in it that you haven't seen a thousand times before.

Bless it for that.

Everything and everybody in this city bid for your attention every second of every day, hack at you and plead with you and insult you until you submit.

What we don't have here is a surfeit of oases.

Trees line the three streets on which the new building sits. While they're spindly still and not too leafy, in a few years they'll be thick and burgeoning, a quiet pleasure. They won't ask us to defer to them; they'll defer to us.

Mediocrity, at its best, is competent and a little shy.

Aren't these the qualities we look for in a neighbor?

Someone who, in an emergency, will call 911 or perform the Heimlich maneuver, and otherwise stay quiet.

Someone who, encountered in the hall or lobby, will ask after our well-being, but insincerely.

In other words, a presence that is almost as welcome as an absence.

The building across the street is going to be a very good neighbor.

About the people inside the building, I shudder to think.

I Completely Agree, But:
Two Nostalgias

Billie was talking about the old Times Square:

"It was fetid, man, it was rank. You couldn't go a block without skidding over some addict's shit or some homeless person's fresh trail of vomit. You took your life in your hands there.

"You had the addicts, you had the pimps, you had the hookers, the *tranny* hookers, the hookers with AIDS.

"You had the homeless, the *homeless* with AIDS.

"Those days were cold, man—those winters!

"You had the porn, the porn bookstores, the porn theaters, the shooting galleries, the glory holes, the killers.

"There were *killers* on those streets. Cold-blooded, pistol-packing, machete-hacking—it was crazy! It was *real*.

"You'd go home, you'd be fucked up—you'd seen something—you'd always just seen something, sometimes it'd be a fresh corpse, I tell no lie: this newly dead form on the street!

"And you'd get on the subway and you'd get to your apartment, and you were on fire!

"You were making art! You were sizzling with art! You were literally making art to save your life, you were burning up with that shit. People were getting murdered, man, they were getting *murdered*."

Billie, who, it goes without saying, belongs to that lucky remnant, the unmurdered who got to make the art, shook her head.

"Now you go there—well, you don't go there. All that Disney. That Disney shit. It's not even a place anymore. It's a non-place.

"Back then, the eighties, man. We were on fire. We were burning up. None of this family shit. None of this clean-ass shit. None of this Goofy and Daffy crap.

"We were dying—we were *alive*."

She misses those days badly.

But this is nostalgia for plague.

James could only dream of a time before he was born:

"In those days, the players were regular people. They were working stiffs. They weren't millionaires, multimillionaires.

"In the off-season, you'd see them around town. Like, your Hall of Fame shortstop and he'd be changing your oil.

"They *had* to work. This was before Flood and Mitchelson and collective bargaining and free agency.

"This was before they all became mercenaries.

"They didn't make enough money then to carry them through the off-season. They were gas jockeys. They were carpenters.

"They were part of your town, you could say hi to them.

"The team was the same team year after year—you grew up with these guys, you cared about them, you identified with them.

"It's not like now where it's what Fortune 500 company am I rooting for?

"They were *people*.

"You were a *community*.

"You cared.

"You can't care anymore.

"Not if you think about it.

"If you think about it, it's disgusting.

"The thing Steinbrenner said that time? 'If I want to look at millionaires, I'll go into my locker room.'

"That's just sad.

"It's freaking sad.

"It's not even really summer anymore."

He looked off to the side. He was picturing those lazy hazy crazy days he never got to have.

Which is nostalgia for feudalism.

Local Character

I'm going to go slowly here because I'm still working this out and I may not have all the information.

There was a time when places had what was known as Local Character.

No particular value was placed on this quality because nobody had any choice in the matter.

These were the days before the majestic cargo ships and high-speed locomotives and carrier trucks.

If your town was near well-stocked waters, yours was a fishing community.

If you were surrounded by verdant fields, you were farmers.

Local character was a matter of limitations, sometimes of scarcity.

Then the Industrial Revolution came, along with the revolution in transportation (I'm skipping a little), and the limitations faded.

Eventually, almost every place had access to almost everything, and local character diminished.

Cities began to resemble one another, and if you traveled among them, it could be disorienting. There was a kind of spatial aphasia to it—the right buildings in the wrong relationships.

It was like getting lost while driving in Orange County, California. You see a strip mall and think you're on track again, then look up and a skyscraper you recognize is incorrectly situated. That's because this strip mall isn't your strip mall, it's its near-identical twin, and you're no closer to where you meant to be than you were when you knew you were hopelessly lost.

People lament the loss of local character, which, as it vanishes, grows proportionately dear.

I lament the loss of local character, the homogenization of everything.

Movements arise to preserve the indigenous aspects of a place.

This is where things get confusing.

Because once you have to fight to preserve the character of a place, the character of the place is, by definition, no longer a necessity. And its character was born of necessity. It reflected what nature provided and how society was organized.

So, if you are successful in your bid to preserve the indigenous, *have* you actually preserved it?

Or have you rendered it quaint?

It's possible that what you're left with is just a version of Celebration, Florida—that community that was built by taking scenic facades from old Hollywood movies and slapping houses on the back of them in the hope of inducing *It's a Wonderful Life*.

Yet so much of the new stuff, the cookie-cutter stuff, is soul-crushingly awful.

I suppose we can look forward to the upcoming resource wars.

Mobility will be limited, scarcity will return, and places will start to feel like themselves again.

Weatherless Chelsea

In Chelsea, we get very little weather. This is not a frequent topic of conversation among the residents, though if you mention it, everyone concurs. I first brought it up with Alan of Alan's Alley, the video store that used to be on Ninth Avenue between Twenty-Second and Twenty-Third. He's a nice man and I thought he'd be lenient when he realized what a crackpot I was. Instead, he nodded and said, "It's very peculiar."

My friend Leslie recently met a young woman on the subway, under the kind of circumstances in which strangers start talking to each other—a power outage or something like that. The woman said she'd been living in Chelsea for a year. "I hear you don't get weather there," Leslie said to her. "It's the most peculiar thing," the woman agreed.

I've thought of using my connections to get in touch with a few of the more attractive local TV meteorologists and have them explain the phenomenon to me. But I don't have any connections.

You're not allowed to live in New York City unless you're a noted theorist specializing in everything so everyone has a hypothesis. The river. The angle of the sun. Something about deliquescence. These are not helpful suggestions.

Our lack of weather, curiously, does not spare us the catastrophic effects of weather. In the hours before Hurricane Sandy blasted everything, Chelsea, a few blocks east of the river, saw a light mist, yet ours was one of the last neighborhoods in Manhattan to have its power restored. By way of contrast, on the Upper West Side, where there are frequently typhoons while Chelsea still yearns for drizzle, the power never went out.

My guess is that there are innumerable microclimates in the city—they may be as prolific as stars—as well as climates that last only a moment. My friend Debbie was in one of those a few years ago.

She had paused for a Don't Walk sign when a cloud broke directly over her head. It was a bespoke deluge; when it was over—it lasted about ten seconds—she looked at the squares of pavement to the right and left of the square she was standing on, behind her, and at the street in front of her: all bone-dry. It was a Jobian experience. She had been singled out for abuse as a test—but of what? When she crossed the street, gawking passersby slid out of her way, fearing contagion.

Another time, Debbie was running late for an appointment and was stopped for a Don't Walk sign on an island in the middle of Park Avenue. She turned to the woman on her left and asked for the time. "It's two twenty-five," said Jacqueline Onassis. Debbie went into a fugue state. She saw that tragic motorcade, the bloodied pink suit, three-year-old John John's devastating salute to his father's coffin. She barely knew what she was doing when the light changed and she crossed the street.

I realize this last story has nothing to do with the weather, but I thought you'd like to know how interesting Debbie's life is when she isn't walking.

As I Was Saying to
Kitty Genovese

Every Saturday at two a.m., there's an eruption of human noise on Ninth Avenue, in the Chelsea section. Mocking laughter. "Fuck"-laced accusations. Explicit threats. Treble-clef screams from women not in imminent danger. This happens like clockwork. You wonder about the bona fides of an id that unleashes its furies so punctually.

This is a traveling mayhem; there are clubs a few blocks west where disorder goes to fuel up, and Friday is their busy night. Still, it makes me sad to think that even those behaviors that boil at the far edge of civility have something pre-cast about them, that it may not be rage we're being treated to but the imitation, even the emulation, of rage.

One night last October, it was a different story. First of all, it was four o'clock, not two, when I was awakened, and the noise that jolted me from sleep did not emerge from the usual registers. I wasn't sure people were involved at all. It was like the opening line of *Gravity's Rainbow*: a screaming came across the sky. I lay in bed and listened until the sound fragmented and became intelligible. It was a human noise, after all, and it was arranged in words. There were two men at the base of it and they were using that portion of their voices we don't generally realize we have, the range that's reserved for homicide—the wish, if not the act. I got out of bed and went into the small sitting room that's on the other side of my bedroom and stood in the window. Fourteen floors down, two brothers were having at it. I knew by then that they were brothers because one of the sentences they kept repeating in their chapped, high, horrific voices, each in his turn, was "You're my fucking brother!" Sometimes it was expanded to "How can you fucking *do* this? You're my fucking brother!" I found myself rethinking my opinion of kitchen-sink realism. Those plays had been on the money.

The two brothers were conducting their war on the sidewalk that fronts a short block of small, awninged restaurants and cafés and one paint store. At the corner, which is the southwest corner, stands a Korean deli, which was open and blazing light. Its outdoor stalls of flowers and fruits and vegetables looked imperiled by the brothers' distemper, but the physical violence they were intent on doing was reserved for each other. There was a car parked in front of them, it was theirs, and one or the other of them, at intervals, would open the driver's-side door and get in, only to be immediately dragged out by the other pulling hard on the would-be driver's arm, hard enough to dislodge the arm from its socket, I thought. Then the verbal barrage would continue. At four o'clock on Saturday mornings, the traffic on Ninth Avenue is light but swift. The brothers kept shoving each other into it. This was not a gesture that hedged its bets. Sometimes the brother who was being pushed would lose his balance and teeter farther into the avenue. There were near misses with the speeding cars and none of them had the effect of modifying the men's behavior. They really were out to kill. I watched this for quite a while. I couldn't believe how long it was going on, and there was the thrill of seeing in real life the sort of thing I had seen only in movies and on television, and been bored by.

Finally, it occurred to me that I might have some responsibility in this situation. There was no question that I had a role in it: I was a witness. The key to making bystander apathy work for you is the presence of others to absorb your obligation. There were pitifully few others to be found that morning. When one came along, I treasured that person and tried to pick up a cue from him or her. It seemed significant that the two or three people who passed on the sidewalk, walking from an unseen point south of the skirmish to an unseen point north of it, did not alter their gait because of it. They didn't speed up or walk in loops. They didn't hunch into themselves or stare fixedly down at the sidewalk, either. This suggested that my take on the event was exaggerated. At ground level, this all might look like nothing worse than a sloppy moment between drunks. Still, I thought, what would it hurt to call 911? I could go upstairs where my phone is and give a report filigreed with caveats and provisos. It *seems* a serious altercation, I could say. There is *some* pushing into traffic. Should there *be* a squad car in the vicinity, it *might* be a good idea to have a look. I could sound like an Englishman. I don't know why I didn't do this. Possibly I feared I'd be asked to give my name. I never give my name unless forced to. I dislike consequences of any kind, and all actions seem to me to precede catastrophes. Something kept me still. What if one brother did have the timing to get the other one killed? No one would know I'd witnessed it. And if anyone had seen me witnessing it, that person would probably not be able to identify me or point out which window was mine and would, in any event, be equally culpable and unlikely to report me for that reason.

But what if gradually, over months—over years—that theoretical other witness was flooded with a Dostoyevskyan guilt and took us both down? What if I were the one with the Dostoyevskyan guilt? There'd be every sort of self-destructive behavior indicated, and I have the tools for those. I decided I would give the brothers five more minutes, then make the call.

I'd looked away while I was having these thoughts.

When I looked back, something had changed. There was no more yelling or shoving. The two brothers were easing into the car, in the regular way, one into the driver's seat, the other into the passenger's seat. They swung their shoulder straps smoothly into the buckles and drove off nicely, not burning rubber. My services had not been required after all.

It's such a vexing question: If you had been an ordinary (untargeted) citizen of Nazi Germany, what would you have done? I'm pretty sure I know the answer to that one. What I'm not sure is whether I consider myself lucky that I've been endowed with—or developed on my own—a knack for not getting tested.

Here, Too, Is New York

Hard to believe it's been more than a decade since New York was hit with an epidemic of *The Gates*.

Ground Zero was Central Park, but it spread to all five boroughs and farther, into the tristate area and beyond.

Practically nobody wasn't vulnerable.

You'd be with your irascible, merciless, slashing friends—good, fun people—and you'd see That Look.

A kind of beatitude.

And you knew they'd been felled by it.

The Gates was an installation, the work of the Belgian artist Christo and his French wife, Jean-Claude, whose collaborative shtick was to wrap extremely large objects like the Eiffel Tower in material.

What they did ten years ago was this: they set up goalposts or stanchions or whatever snaking through 23 or 46 or 749 miles of Central Park and from the top of them they hung large rectangles of fabric. The single most controversial aspect of these objects qua objects was the name of the color of the fabric.

The artists said it was saffron, but to many who saw only orange, this seemed like a case of nouveau-riche upstart labeling.

Saffron is the world's most expensive spice—it's the stamens of crocuses and has to be handpicked by the oppressed and a quarter ounce of it can set you back fifteen bucks—whereas orange is the color of traffic cones and Creamsicles.

I never made it to *The Gates* myself—I'm sure they were transcendent—but my one psychotic break in regard to them came around this issue.

A friend who'd just Seen Them stopped by with That Look and started waxing lyrical about their "luscious saffron color," at which point I found it necessary to explain:

"THEY'RE NOT FUCKING SAFFRON, OKAY? THEY'RE ORANGE! LOOK! I HAVE SOME SAFFRON RIGHT HERE. SEE IT? NOW LET'S DO A SEARCH FOR *THE GATES*. THERE THEY ARE! DO THEY LOOK LIKE THIS SAFFRON TO YOU? NO, THEY DON'T! AND YOU KNOW WHY? BECAUSE THEY'RE OR-ANGE! *GET* IT? NOT SAFFRON, ORANGE! NOT SAF-FRON, *ORANGE*!"

She didn't get it; she was too far gone.

This is a thing that happens from time to time in New

York City: the populace gets body-snatched by An Event. The Event turns into an imperative and people who don't make it there in a timely fashion start visibly to diminish; it's like a physical wasting.

And they grow pale, so very pale.

Every now and then you'd run across someone who wasn't susceptible.

My sister-in-law, who can be useful at times like these, walked past them and said, "Give me a break."

My friend Ricky thought they looked like the entrance to the world's largest Home Depot.

Saying that kind of thing could land you in deep trouble.

You were likely to find yourself in the presence of someone like that fancy lady in the *New York Times* who, when someone near her had the temerity to admit he didn't see what the big deal was, turned to a stranger she assumed would be complicit and announced: "Barbarian at the Gates."

Hahahahahahahahahahahahahahahahahahahahaha!

Mostly, though, you'd see a lot of people walking around the city with a Childlike Sense of Wonder.

I'm Jewish, and for me it was like that thing that happens one Wednesday every year when I can't figure out why so many people's foreheads are dirty.

Why was everybody looking so confused?

Oh right: they'd just been to *The Gates*.

They were deep into their internal monologue, which went like this:

Oh, I feel such a childlike sense of wonder. Or do I feel a childlike sense of wonder? I wonder if it's possible I no longer can feel a childlike sense of wonder? No, I'm pretty sure I feel a childlike sense of wonder.

Then they'd bump into something.

New Yorkers are multi-taskers, and they became good at shoehorning this transfiguration into their schedules. "Okay," they'd say, "so we'll meet up at Pain Quotidien for nosh, then you have the orthodontist, I'll browse through Bergdorf's, then we'll go to *The Gates* and be transfigured, then you can stop at Staples and pick up the new printer, I'll go to Schatzie's for a brisket and home in time for *Jeopardy.*"

A few celebrities demurred. Keith Olbermann said they screwed up the view from his Central Park South apartment. But people who have views from Central Park South apartments are not sympathetic figures.

On average, it was a religion.

The Gates were officially over weeks before they were torn down. My friend Linda was walking through the park during this time, her childlike sense of wonder in tow, when she stumbled across an elderly Frenchwoman who was smiling at her. It was Jean-Claude!

"You like?" said Jean-Claude, or something in that vein.

Linda allowed as how she liked very much. And Jean-Claude, who took to Linda immediately—everybody takes to Linda immediately—picked up a bit of orange fabric that had been taken from one of the flags and encased in plastic and, in a gesture like a benediction, handed it to her (and those samples were going for a pretty penny at that point).

Linda showed me the rag as if it were a cutting from the Shroud of Turin.

"Isn't that the most beautiful saffron?" she said.

"It certainly is," I said back.

When I moved to the city in the mid-eighties, the disease going around was a foreign film called *My Life as a Dog*.

Nobody could get over *My Life as a Dog*.

It was playing at the Lincoln Plaza Cinemas, which back then was an obnoxious place to go. It was a multiplex of tiny auditoriums—there were seven or eight movies playing at a time—and after you bought your ticket, tall, thin, yellow-haired ushers in black would force you into labyrinthine lines that had been arranged confusingly to bear no perceptible relationship to the theaters they allegedly fed into. If you misbehaved in your line—if you tried to duck under the rope for a quick trip to the bathroom or moved as though you were planning to make a break for it and head for your auditorium without permission, the ushers chastised you severely. They were intent on giving you the full stalag experience. None of the *My Life as a Dog* people minded because they knew that at the end of their ordeal waited *My Life as a Dog*.

It was all anybody talked about.

"Movies are terrible now," said your waiter. "But have you seen *My Life as a Dog*?"

"I'm still in a kind of trance from *My Life as a Dog*," your dentist admitted over the novocaine.

"So sad about Izzie," said the mourners at the funeral, "but you *must* see *My Life as a Dog*."

My Life as a Dog! *My Life as a Dog*!—there was no getting away from it.

Finally I caved. I saw *My Life as a Dog*.

It was okay.

Here's an Idea

New York City is now in the business of erecting abandoned buildings. The most notorious one is on West Fifty-Seventh Street. It is ninety or so stories high and casts a broad and permanent shadow over Central Park. Its apartments go for tens of millions of dollars and are to be owned by Russian oligarchs and magnates from the Arab Emirates who will visit from time to time but not sleep in these apartments more than twenty nights a year.

Through my window, I can see one of these buildings near Chelsea Piers. It is terribly, effacingly tall and was designed by an immensely famous architect who clearly wasn't trying. You cannot believe how ordinary it is. Nevertheless, its units are selling for fifteen and twenty and forty million dollars and include all the amenities: bedrooms by the dozen, bowling lanes, wine cellars, atriums, screening rooms, en suite carports, and swimming pools.

One of them has already been snapped up by an oligarch

or a magnate—in any event, a very rich foreigner—who is, I think, insane. This is why I think so:

Like many of the plutocrats who drop thirty or forty mil on living spaces they have no intention of living in, this one bought it without ever seeing the place, which was, in fact, not yet fully built when he made the purchase. He relied on descriptions, illustrations, elevations, and his personal real estate scout, a former Cockney named Neville.

Neville touted the beauty of the layout, the spaciousness of the carport, the Olympic dimensions of the swimming pool, and the panoramic breadth of the view. By day's end, a check was cut.

What happened next was, the magnate made a quick trip to New York and stopped in on his new acquisition, which by then was far enough along that it had staircases, though the staircases still lacked bannisters. Neville accompanied him and left, it's safe to say, shy a ball or two.

He had neglected to tell his boss that what the panoramic view was of was Hoboken, New Jersey.

This did not make the new owner feel house-proud. As a foreigner, he lacked a textured understanding of the city and its environs, and was unaware that in the opinion of the cognoscenti, Hoboken was almost as ritzy as Astoria. He stewed about this situation all through the very long and lonely trip on the private plane back to Dubai or wherever. What was he to do? It wasn't as if he could flip a forty-million-dollar apartment.

Then it hit him.

You can check this out on Facebook:

He is petitioning the Port Authority of New York and New Jersey to install a fifty-story mirror at the western edge of the Hudson River to run the length of the High Line.

"At these prices," he writes, "I deserve to be looking at something worth looking at."

Last I visited, the petition had more than three thousand signatures.

I'm sure some of them are satirical.

In the Moment

These days a lot of spiritual prestige is accorded to being in the moment, and I have to admit, by that standard, I fare very well. I am always in the moment. The moment I'm in happens to have taken place fifty years ago, but I see no reason that should count against me. The important thing is that I'm profoundly *in it*, very, very present.

You can see me there, if you'd like. I'm with Marlo Thomas as she twirls her parasol and her liquid brown eyes scan a sea of Broadway-neon marquees touting such delectable offerings as *The Star Spangled Girl* and *Funny Girl* and *There's a Girl in My Soup*. I am deeply concerned about LBJ's Southeast Asia policy and I am planning a decorating scheme. I'm seven but motivated.

Forty years later, I implemented the decorating scheme. The look of my apartment was up-to-the-minute if you were Dean Martin. I threw a party to celebrate. My friend Debbie was there. Debbie believes life is a romantic comedy set in Manhattan; certain neighborhoods only. Once, I asked her if she thought my temperament was too retrospective, and she said, "You're asking *me* that? I stop at World War Two." I stood in the vestibule of my apartment and took in the party and was quite sure that Comden and Green, both long dead, were in attendance, or at least giving their ghostly blessing. Such color! Such life! So many witty people, one or two of them famous! A river view! Everything but the cigarette smoke! "It is, isn't it?" I said to Debbie. "It's *Bells Are Ringing*."

Even Debbie hesitated a fraction. "Yes," she said with conviction plus something less than conviction.

The problem with planning your life for a very long time is that when happiness finally comes, it's outmoded.

My Racial Incident

I was involved in a racial incident at my corner Rite Aid the other day.

It was my father's ninety-sixth birthday and I had gone to buy candles for the cupcakes we were bringing him. Because it was a small purchase, I decided to pay with cash. The woman at the cash register, an African American woman who had never appeared to like her job (and why should she?), forked over the change. I thought it was short five cents but I moved on anyway.

Taking a few steps toward the exit, I inspected the change in my hand. Coins seem to get altered without notice and I considered the possibility that what looked like a smallish nickel was in fact some new largish dime. It wasn't. I had been shortchanged.

Even though I happened to be strapped at the moment, five cents were not going to effect a change in my condition. I could easily have let the error pass, and if I had made it to the street before discovering the discrepancy, I would have.

But something about the blatancy of the mistake, and having seen it as it was happening—and being steps away from where I could get it corrected—made me not want to let it go. To do so seemed too dweebishly liberal, weak, and, in some obscure way, patronizing.

The cashier was attending to a customer and a short line had formed to the left of the register. I stood to the right and waited for the transaction to be completed.

As I waited, the cashier noticed me and gave me a slightly affronted, frankly questioning look. It was not a glance, it was a fixed look. So I said, "Oh, you actually owe me five cents."

She thrust out her hand for me to present the evidence. I stepped forward and gave her the receipt with my right hand and showed her the change in my left.

As she studied the receipt, she said, "For the next time, you should know you're being very rude to the other customer."

This threw me. Quickly, I apologized to the lady who had been interrupted. She was a slender black woman, about forty. She shrugged it off; it was clearly no big deal to her.

Then I said to the cashier, "I thought you'd finished helping her."

This was a mistake. In the first place, it wasn't what I meant. It was something concise to say on the spot. What I meant was: I was standing politely to the side. You gave me a look that demanded an answer. I answered. I was mild—in no way insisting on immediate redress of my grievance. You might very well have said—you should have said—"Let me finish with this customer first." Obviously, I wasn't going to make a fuss.

No—"I thought you'd finished helping her" had not been a well-judged remark, and when the cashier heard it, she gave me a look of scorn and incredulity. Reflexively, I apologized a second time to the other customer, who, this time, was not happy to hear it. She blocked me out. A smothered sigh escaped from her. I sensed she was tired of being asked to absolve white people when all she wanted was to buy a roll of paper towels or some fabric softener.

I was handed my nickel. I did not receive an apology for the original error, something I'd thought would come automatically. I made it quickly out of there and took a cab to my father's apartment.

Here is the situation as I see it: I was shortchanged; I behaved properly; I did all the apologizing.

Though this happened three days ago, I haven't been able to stop thinking about it, and the more I unpack it, the more loaded it seems to be.

[**CITY FRIENDS**]

Trapped

Most of the people I know feel trapped. What I don't know is whether there's statistical value to this observation or if it's only a function of me. It's possible that I have eliminated from my life the people I once knew who are not trapped, out of resentment of their status. Even more likely is that carefree people want nothing to do with me.

Most of the trapped people I know were not trapped when I first met them or, if they were, had colorful tales to tell of the high-flying times they'd had before they were. Most of these bountiful times involved money, fortunes of money. Fortunes of money are false predictors, and many of the people I know who had fortunes of money and are now trapped believed this false prediction and cite the profligate behavior that stemmed from this belief as the source of their entrapment. The people who live with a memory of money generally believe that if their money could be miraculously restored to them, they would no longer feel trapped. What they are forgetting is their corollary losses. Health and hope and youth and friendships have also fallen by the wayside and these are even harder to replenish than the exchequer. It's easier to dwell on the money because money is hard and quantifiable and as such makes an excellent fetish object.

It's very much like being overweight. People who are fat have only one problem until they become thin and discover they have thousands.

My Friend,
the Murderer Manqué

I met a friend for coffee at the diner late this afternoon.

This diner used to be a different diner or, more accurately, as neither menu nor ownership has changed, the same diner with a different name, floor plan, and style of décor.

In the old days, it was one marvelously ugly room, L-shaped, in tones of gray and puce, and it featured spacious partitioned booths where you could sit for hours; they were like sublets. Back then, the place was always packed.

The booths have been junked for narrower booths, along the sides of the room only, and in the center are ranks of tables and chairs packed closely but not oppressively so. The look is, I would say, West Coast retro, with dangling lamps over the booths and tomato-colored walls. It's very nearly good-looking and the seating capacity has almost doubled. Nobody goes there anymore.

The emptiness of the place—near emptiness, that is—is crucial to what happened there this afternoon.

The friend I was meeting has the kind of sonorous voice you often hear among men who *trained* to be actors but didn't *get* to be actors. It's a voice that dominates and travels and invests his every mundane remark with a quality of self-congratulation. Because of this, strangers and casual acquaintances often think he's an asshat. He's not an asshat, really; he just has all this resonance and nothing to do with it. I would ask him to lower his voice, only how can you ask someone something like that? What I do instead is lower my own voice, first to near inaudibility, then to total inaudibility, in the hope that the level will prove infectious. It never does.

Today, as I mentioned, the place was only seemingly empty—there were in truth a few patrons scattered throughout the room as well as a large contingent of waiters milling about or just standing guard. There were, in other words, enough people to bear ear-witness to my friend's monologue but not enough to drown it out or absorb the sound of it in their bodies, and the walls, exposed to one another, formed an echo chamber.

This was what he told me:

"I could never be a murderer—I don't have the gumption for it—but more and more my present situation is leading me to understand the logic of murder."

I just looked at him. He went on.

"Say you are yoked to someone—and it's a lifelong yoke—with whom your relations have always been shabby and brutal. And, as is so often the case with brutal people, this brutal person has no intention of ever dying.

"He has accrued untold years and while there has never been love between you, and scarcely even civility, he has fallen to you as your life's burden.

"Now you've reached a point yourself when old age is peeping over the horizon—you've had your scares, your health problems—and you know you're in the last phase of life where things might get better.

"But while for you the prospect of old age represents a shriveling, for him it seems an infinitely elastic proposition—eternal!

"Not that he hasn't diminished. He has, badly.

"He now comprises sleep, ingestion, bad temper, and incontinence.

"Oh, and crisis.

"Crises timed like eggs, to crop up whenever you might be enjoying a pleasant moment or making strategies for yourself.

"And these are all you have—these pleasant moments and strategies for escape.

"And to make it worse, this brutal person doesn't even really want to live himself—he just hasn't figured out how not to; it's this habit he can't break. If only there were a Lived-Too-Long Anonymous!

"But as long as he keeps doing it, you have to keep supporting it—and because of what?

"Convention. Sentimentality. The Law. The Horror of the Opinion of People Who Do Not Understand!

"Well, it's only natural at this point that you start to think of people as economies.

"Economies of time. Economies of money.

"His versus yours.

"And it hammers at you that this person—who destroyed your childhood, afflicted your youth, and blights your middle age—is all set up for no good reason to rob you of your old age and scant resources as well.

"Hours and dollars. Dollars and hours.

"And this is how the murderer sees it, isn't it?

"And very understandably so, I might add.

"Yesterday, a friend was over for breakfast, someone from California I never see. I got a call. There'd been a social services interruption—there always are these social services interruptions—they hire these people from the lumpen proletariat exclusively.

"He needed to be visited and brought food.

"This was the grocery list: frankfurters, frankfurter buns, cupcakes, and cream cheese.

"Truly, that was the list.

"I went to Gristedes—how did that guy, that Catsimatidis, who owns that chain ever think he could be elected mayor? Doesn't he know there isn't a New Yorker alive who hasn't *smelled* a Gristedes?—anyway, I went.

"Next to the regular frankfurters there were low-sodium frankfurters.

"I thought: 'He won't be able to tell the difference between the low-sodium and the regular.'

"And I put two packages of the regular frankfurters in my carry bag.

"Next to the full-fat cream cheese there was a low-fat option.

"I thought, 'He won't be able to tell the difference between low-fat and full-fat.'

"And I put the full-fat in my carry bag.

"In the bakery section I found cupcakes that looked to have been frosted with a glue gun.

"And this was the parcel I brought to my nemesis.

"There was intention to my choices, to be sure. But I don't think they'll get me into any kind of trouble, will they?

"Or *will* they?

"The law can be so *nuanced* these days."

He stared at me.

The sparsely populated but not unpopulated room had gone rigid listening, or so it seemed to me.

I looked away, out the window.

I find unusual things romantic, and the scene that presented itself out the window hit my sweet spot. It was almost dark, a cold November darkness, and people were walking quickly home, their collars turned up against the wind, some visibly shivering. Lights were starting in the apartment windows—warm ambers—and I imagined I could smell the beginnings of family dinners, of roasting meats and baking crumbles. I am sharply nostalgic for things that I wish had happened, and normally, really on any given day, I would have found the scene piercing and enjoyable, but today, it made me think of chaos and rage, of murderous nannies and the dispossessed.

I turned back to my friend.

He was done with his afternoon's talking and his eyes looked sad and pleading.

"But you *don't* have the gumption, right?" I asked him at long last.

"No," he said wistfully and—eureka!—softly.

"I don't have the gumption."

Surprising Friend

From time to time, I find the constraints of my character suffocating and take on a project simply because it isn't like me.

So it was that I found myself, at a friend's urging, a member of a poetry reading group that met once a month in an apartment on West Twelfth Street.

I've had a sporadic interest in poetry, and for six months in the mid-nineties, I wrote poems myself, wrote them manically, obsessively, in elation. Then I stopped. I thought that would be it for poetry, until the reading group.

In the group was a gob-smackingly handsome young man named Ezekiel (which is not his real name but a name I've never used before and so I'm using it now). He was a hyphenate—actor-model-poet or something like that—in his late twenties or early thirties.

I don't usually seek out the company of gob-smackingly handsome young men—their presence makes me edgy— and though, in theory, there's nothing funnier than a beautiful, tortured dumb guy, Ezekiel, while pretty tortured, was not quite dumb enough to make his entertainment factor offset the jarring qualities of his beauty.

Nevertheless, something about me—my awkwardness, my jokiness, my vocabulary—drew his interest—he thought there was good to be mined from me—and a few months into the workshop, we made a date to meet at my local diner and discuss Gerard Manley Hopkins and sprung rhythm.

The evening got off to an only mildly uncomfortable start. Ezekiel's beautiful slate-gray eyes are seeking eyes, and seeking eyes always make me feel as though there's nothing to be found in me. But once we'd read to each other the poem "Heaven-Haven: A Nun Takes the Veil," a rhythm established itself and I began to think things would go surprisingly well.

It was then that Ezekiel got a text.

I've never texted in my life—I fear the consequence of arthritic thumbs—so I am reverential in the presence of the texts of others.

Ezekiel looked at me apologetically, that searching look.

There was an emergency.

"Is everything all right?" I asked.

"It's not a health thing—but I've got to go. Would you wait? It might take a while."

This diner being the one public place where I feel comfortable alone, I told him that I would wait gladly. Off he went, and I sat sipping coffee and reading Hopkins as well as other books I'd brought along in a bag I sometimes carry. Also I wrote. It was quite pleasant.

Two hours later, Ezekiel returned.

His hair was wet—I glanced outside; it was a rainless evening—and he smelled freshly showered.

"Um . . . ?" I inquired.

"Yes, yes," he said, all abashed regret.

"I owe you an explanation." He took a deep breath. "I had a date."

"I'm sorry . . . a date?"

"Yes."

"An emergency *date*?"

"Not that kind of a date."

And he looked at me frankly, as though he had revealed something deeply personal.

I'm not the swiftest horse out of the gate but I'd watched enough police procedurals to figure out what he was talking about.

"Oh."

"Yes."

"You're even more of a hyphenate than I knew."

"It wasn't something I chose! *It* chose *me*."

Then he explained the manner of his selection.

"I was doing this modeling thing, this photo thing— nude, you know, this nude modeling thing—and we were done and the photographer—I'll call him Jack—was, oh, *pleased* with how the session went, and as I was dressing— well, *before* I was dressing, actually—he hugged me—out of professional gratitude, you know? Not only for that reason, as it turned out, and you know it's my propensity to go where the day takes me; you know, as long as I don't perceive an actual bodily threat—or have an appointment—or anything—so I let him just *keep* hugging me and then he sort of, I don't know, *slid* down my body and, kind of, took me in his mouth? And I thought, Well, yes, well, sure, well, why not? I mean, I didn't have to be anywhere for a while. And he was, um, skilled? And I have to admit it was quite pleasurable, quite an excellent way to spend an unscheduled hour. So he finished—well, I guess you'd have to say *I* finished—and he smiled at me and he looked really grateful, even though, really *I* was the one who'd been serviced. I found that touching, you know? Very, very touching. So he told me where the shower was and I showered and dressed and he gave me an envelope with cash in it. This was surprising and not surprising. *Not* surprising because I'd done a job, there was a fee. But surprising because I'd expected to be paid by check. As I walked out, I counted the money. I sort of half thought maybe there'd be less than I'd been promised because, you know, he'd made another kind of payment, so to speak. But there wasn't. There was five hundred dollars more! At first, I thought maybe it was a mistake, but no, of course it wasn't. And it just seemed so lovely, you know? Like such a lovely *gesture*? And I'm always a little on the broke side, so this extra would come in handy. And then I thought nothing more about it.

"Two days later, Jack called and told me that a dear friend whom he was going to call Paul was in town staying at the Sherry-Netherland and he'd told Paul about me and Paul was interested in meeting me, that afternoon, in fact, if I was free. And it just so happened that I *was* so I said I'd meet him. Then Jack told me that he told Paul my name was Terry, so I should respond to 'Terry.' I'm always interested in cloak-and-dagger things and aliases and stuff like that, so the idea was very pleasing to me. So I met Paul at his suite at the Sherry-Netherland, which was truly stupendous. At that point, I wasn't *sure* why we were getting together, but when I met him, Paul hugged me in a sort of *primal* way? And the thing about Paul was, he had this really intoxicating smell. He smelled like the first day of spring or a newborn after its first bath. I mean, clean beyond our American standards, which, as they are, are very high-normal. And you know, that *delights* me, that makes me feel as if everything in life is good. So we undressed each other and had sex, and after, he pointed me the way to the shower and when I was done showering I went back to the living room, naked, and Paul was gone. He'd folded my clothes really neatly and placed them on a chair and on top of my clothes on the chair was an envelope with my *nom de sexe*, Terry, on it in quotation marks. And in the envelope were nine brand-new hundred-dollar bills.

I didn't think that was obligatory but it wasn't surprising, either. And it turned out Paul had friends, all very interesting, very moneyed, very *hygienic* people, and *they* had friends and it's been like a pyramid and I find it all really extremely fascinating."

"Oh," I said.

We tried going back to Hopkins and sprung rhythm but we never quite found our groove again.

I know there's nothing unusual about Ezekiel's story, or "Terry's"—or Pete's, even. This is New York City and we're all adults, all jades. Still, I can't help feeling that in some muted, old-fashioned way, it remains at least a little shocking.

Especially if you've lived so strictly within the margins, anyone would think the margins were electrified.

Socialism

My friend who understands murder phoned me up at two o'clock last Thursday morning. He's drinking now.

"I have the most breathtaking idea!" he slurred. "Wouldn't it be fantastic if we could socialize time?"

"It's two o'clock in the—"

"Hear me out! Say we could scoop up all those years being thrown away on horrible people who are festering way past their sell-by dates and redistribute them among good people who die young for no reason."

"Yeah, that's a nice idea—but it's two o'clock in the—"

"Don't patronize me! Are you saying you'd be *against* this if it meant your lovely friend Jill could still be here? Or Ileen? Or Fredda? Or Dorie? Can you honestly *say* that?"

"No, I can't."

Worst-Case Scenarios

Lately, I've been picking up a little extra cash writing worst-case scenarios.

The couple who hired me to do this are longtime friends with a thirteen-year-old daughter who has been too passionately embracing the freedom of the city.

My friends know this is a timely development. It's right that their daughter be left alone and be let to travel alone, but they're terrified that they haven't crippled her with a sufficient sense of anxiety, and in the brightest spirit possible, she has been finding ways around them when they've tried to levy the last custodial restrictions they feel entitled to.

She's a very happy girl. Her darkness has no goblins in it and the stranger lurking behind the pillar is just a friend she hasn't met yet.

To deter her, I've been writing things like this:

With the drastic budget cuts the city has suffered, mental patients are being released from government-funded hospitals at an alarming rate. This has led to a situation where subway platforms citywide are littered with schizophrenics whose idea of a good time is to shove young girls who are leaning too far forward *directly* into the path of oncoming trains. Their schizophrenia has only improved their timing. YOU *WILL* BE HIT.

It's no wonder they asked me to do this—given my habit of mind, this sort of thing doesn't count as writing so much as writing *down*—but I'm ambivalent about the job. It seems a creepy thing to do and, worse, destined to be ineffective.

The world is divided between the fearful and the fancy-free and there's no converting one to the other.

Friendship

The hopelessly thwarted aspiring murderer won't let up. This is what he said to me recently:

"I am constantly trying to torpedo my friendships while maintaining complete deniability."

"Am *I* your friend?" I asked.

"You're one of my *best* friends," he reassured me.

Cute Idea

"You know what would be a cool thing to do?" my murderous friend says: "*Kill* yourself, and in the note, blame it on someone who wronged you in a *totally trivial way*."

[**STORYTELLING**]

My First-World Problem and Go Fuck Yourself

When someone says:

"Do you freaking *believe* it? They didn't send the freaking *limo*? I had to *freaking* call a *freaking* car service and *bill* them? It's freaking apoca*lyp*tic," it is both off-putting and absurd.

On the other hand, this sort of thing:

"But I shouldn't complain. Think how much worse it would be if I had stage four cancer in *Syria*."

while not off-putting is equally absurd.

The trick is to strike a balance.

This is difficult because the words that describe balance have largely been retired from our discourse. If Lionel Trilling were alive, he would exhort us to "modulate," and maybe we would. But he isn't, so no one modulates anymore and it's a damn shame.

The antique word I would like to revive in mitigation of this problem is "seemly."

"Seemly" is an excellent word. To behave in a seemly manner is to understand how you bulk in the scheme of things. It makes room neither for grandiosity nor for that hardening to one's own condition that is a form of moral suicide.

I suspect that only a very limited number of words can be in currency at one time and to wedge in "seemly" we might have to bump off something else.

My candidate is "narrative."

"Narrative" used to be a superb word. I used it myself, often and correctly. What destroyed narrative was the 2008 election; this was because Barack Obama had a "compelling" one.

In short order, politicians developed narrative envy and soon there was an epidemic of narratives. Journalists, in the probing, defeated way they go about their business these days, aggravated the phenomenon by "comparing narratives" instead of doing whatever it is they're supposed to do—reporting on the actual, I suppose.

The essential thing to know about narratives is that they are never accounts of the actual, though to be effective they must have points of contact with it. These points are sifted, curried, and shaped into a fable or, to be mundane, a story.

Stories are treacherous things. That's why if you're in the business of inventing them, you really ought to make them turn on themselves.

Origin Myth

Davey Prather was short, rotund, garrulous, friendly, neurotic, tacitly gay (high school; the seventies) and possessed of a majestic baritone with what in classical singing is called "squillo," or a ringing quality. He did all the high school shows, and the parties after were often held at his house.

His family was a deal. Davey was somewhere in the middle of a pack of twenty or thirty kids, most of whom would make vivid, fleeting appearances at the parties, singly or in sets. Bunches of them were male, tall, glowering, perhaps sociopathic. A few were soubrettes who tossed their hair and giggled and ate fruit in a lubricious manner. Some were whining, some were recessive. Some were sardonic, and some were not different people at all but the same ones you'd seen a minute ago and failed to memorize. It was very hard to get a handle on who was who. The kids appeared to span generations, although when the parents showed up, they always surprised you by being on the youngish side.

The dad was grandfather-clocky, tall and mournful with a slight potbelly where his gong should have been. The mom was a star and everyone was drawn to her. I can't remember if you never saw her without a cigarette or if you never saw her with a cigarette but her voice was unmistakably tobacco-cured, the kind of charismatic rasp that used to cause much comic merriment in movies before everyone started associating the sound with lung cancer and its depredations of pain, facial deformity, and an intubated larynx.

There was always some agitation around her. I remember once Davey wasn't in school and I told my friend Karen the reason I'd been given for his absence.

"His mother is having a hysterectomy."

"*Another* one?" Karen said.

It was like that.

I loved being around the Prathers for the noise they made. My house was stingily populated, and while there was sometimes explosiveness, there was never racket. The Prathers were a passel of simultaneous talkers. Some of what they said, when a sentence wormed its way into an acoustic clearing, was quite shocking; they barracked at each other and you were never sure if it was madcap ribbing or real hatred. They seemed to live on a razor's edge between joy and entropy, but they were alive.

I went through decades trying to figure out what my family stood for, what counted as its animating principle, and the best I could come up with was "Pursue the Path of

Least Resistance." By contrast, a family as loaded as the Prathers has to have an idea of itself, and you couldn't be around them for more than twenty minutes—certainly not around Jean, the mom—before you found out what that idea was.

They had, in fact, an Origin Myth.

You see, it turned out that Davey's voice had not arrived *ex nihil.*

His dad—his name was Martin—had a bass-baritone that left Davey's lashed to the mast. People never heard him sing without crying out, "Chaliapin!" and it was understood that his destiny was to be a great star of the Metropolitan.

Martin himself believed this to be so but was somewhat diffident, or, as we'd put it now, "conflicted."

He'd grown up poor, potato-eatingly poor, and though international stardom was a nice prospect, he had a knack for math, and accountancy or actuarial work beckoned as well, though depressingly.

For a time in the early fifties, in the middle of his era of vacillation, he had a job working as a stagehand on the Milton Berle show, more properly called *Texaco Star Theater.*

Jean was a chorus girl on the program (which, when you found it out, you believed in a second; it seemed impossible that she *wouldn't* have been a chorus girl on that show), and this was the beginning of their courtship.

Everyone wanted Martin to choose Eternal Operatic Stardom because his voice, when he let it out, was a force of nature—women fainted and buildings swayed—but Martin was a fine and dutiful man and it was important to him that whatever he did led to the greatest good for the largest number.

His indecision was beginning to annoy everyone, when an opportunity presented itself.

One week, Uncle Miltie's guest star was to be Ezio Pinza.

Ezio Pinza had been a great operatic bass-baritone. Sadly, today he's best remembered for introducing the turgid ballad "Some Enchanted Evening" in the original production of the morally confused Pulitzer Prize–winning musical *South Pacific*.

At the time, though, he was still an illustrious figure and by all accounts a genial man.

Martin and Jean decided that at some moment during the week of rehearsals, Martin would approach Pinza and ask him to listen to Martin sing, then advise him as to whether he should pursue an operatic career.

The understanding was that after four or five bars, Pinza would cry out, "*Ragazzo! Tu* are *magnifico!* You must drop *tutti altri cosi* at once and *canta, canta, canta!* I will introduce you to Signor Bing *io stesso pronto!*"

The moment came. A break was called, and magically, Martin had a clear shot at Pinza, who even looked somewhat at loose ends, as though he'd welcome the interruption.

Martin had taken a breath, stepped toward Pinza, and

opened his mouth to say, "Signor Pinza," when he was short-stopped by the stage manager, who in the rushing, garbled way of stage managers, tolled, "Signor Pinza! You're wanted in wardrobe!" And off Pinza went to be clothed.

And that was that. The end of everything.

The twenty-year career at the Met. *Boris Godunov* at La Scala. The lengthy Deutsche Grammophon discography.

Martin would go on to a long solvent life of siring children and doing sad actuarial work, but he would never sing again.

All because that stage manager happened to step in at that moment.

"Isn't that something?" Jean would say, nodding with wry and fatalistic wisdom.

The thread from which a life depends.

Okay.

Even at seventeen, I thought there was something fishy about that story. What about initiative? What about spunk? Why not knock on Pinza's dressing room door? Why not drop him a note? Or the hell with Pinza, why not just audition?

But I suspect none of my (silent) objections matter.

The most important thing is to have a story. Because unless you have a story, you're a boat without a sail.

Genre/Role

It isn't always so bad to know what your genre is; in fact, many of us encourage it, canting our lives this way or that, tailoring our patter to ensure that the genre we end up installed in is the one that we want. So that, for example, Sebastian Junger gets to be Epic-Heroic; my friend Debbie is Romantic-Comedic; many of us have settled into Melodrama. And we understand our categories and are comfortable in them.

The mickey comes later, when you've passed some silent meridian, in the thick of life but with a broad view of the thinning side, and you start to suspect that the role you've been assigned *within* your genre is not the one you'd hoped for. What's more, you finally *get* that History happens twice, first as Tragedy, then as Farce, then as Tragedy, then as Farce, then as Tragedy, then as Farce, ad infinitum, the same handful of plots, invariant, the only thing differing from generation to generation the names of the actors plugged into the concrete-cast roles.

Perhaps this makes you think of Ruth Hale, who, at a party one night shortly after the publication of *The Great Gatsby*, went up to its editor, the legendary Max Perkins, and said, "That new book by your *enfant terrible* is really *terrible*," and felt wonderful about herself. Here she was in a roomful of the cleverest people of her time, and she'd got off the best line. Not only had she got off the best line, she'd scored against the annoyingly sterling Max Perkins himself. And a little while later she walked off into the night and looked cornily up at the stars and saw herself twinkling among the constellations, because she had done it, hers was the quote that everyone would be quoting and, as its originator, she'd carved herself a place in the tricky New York firmament. Now she would be spoken of alongside Dorothy Parker. Then she would run roughshod over Dorothy Parker. And it would all just grow and grow and grow and get better and better and better. And ninety years later the only thing Ruth Hale is remembered for is that incredibly fatuous remark.

What if that's you?

What if, in the middle of your High Comedy life, having meant to be Dorothy Parker, you've ended up Ruth Hale instead?

What if, right there in the shimmering ballroom, you're the bitter one, the loveless one, the mocked one, the talentless one, the freak, the suicide?

Genres are nothing; it's the role that damns you.

Rich People

Honestly, I have known some perfectly tolerable rich people.

Warm, brainy, searching, generous rich people, whom it's not a tribulation to talk with.

I've also known some others.

Those ones who seemingly have modeled themselves on the rich people who used to show up in the kind of crappy movies that starred Rodney Dangerfield.

Once, at a party, I was talking to some new rich person, and it seemed to be going well enough. I'd assumed my special party demeanor: courteous, engaged. I had just said something—I don't remember what—sagacious and appropriate, to which this rich person's response was:

"Not dressed like *that* you won't."

When she'd just moved to New York, my friend Linda was at a party on the Upper East Side. Her daughter, who was visiting from out of town, was there, too. They were talking to some new rich people, when in answer to one rich person's question, Linda's daughter said, "I come from Georgia."

"Oh my," that rich person said. "Do you speak English?"

It's a mistake to assume that money has made these people lose their humanity. You become human over time and some of these who were born rich never took on the project. They didn't have to; money was their version of being human. Also their version of Decent Behavior and of Having an Informed Opinion. (Listening to one of these pontificate about Art can give you lockjaw.)

I can't pretend these ones are a deeply concerning issue for me, except for this: I'm not supposed to write about them.

That's because, as a writer who generally works in realism, I'm charged with creating "rounded" characters.

And these are flat people.

Only stupid Rodney Dangerfield–ish movies are allowed to get them right.

Selling Out

As an artist, I am incapable of selling out.

I know because I've failed at it so many times.

God knows my failure hasn't been for lack of stick-to-it-iveness, and I've been willing to genre-hop in the quest to prostitute myself. I've written lots of screenplays and TV pilots; no one's ever put them into production. A few years ago, I noticed that every weekend there opened another movie based on a Nicholas Sparks novel. How hard could it be to write a Nicholas Sparks novel? I reasoned. I went on Amazon and ordered the cheapest one with the fewest pages. It arrived two days later. The first line was "The summer I turned seventeen, everything changed forever."

I was out.

That I encountered problems in my efforts to write lucrative crap shouldn't have surprised me. Nora Ephron diagnosed the situation over forty years ago in an essay semi-defending Jacqueline Susann. Susann's novel *Valley of the Dolls* sold more copies than the Bible, leading literary writers to assume noms de plume and imitate it, never successfully. The difference, Ephron explained, was that they were just "slumming at the typewriter," while Jackie really meant it.

She was doing the best she could.

Sincerity turns out to be the great divider, and not only at the potboiler level. By rights, *It's a Wonderful Life* should be a piece of nauseous sentimentality. That it isn't, is because the director, Frank Capra—an artist far more gifted than Jacqueline Susann—believed every frame of it. It's a work as detailed as a fresco by Leonardo. You can't fake that.

Even so, I'm going to keep trying. What do you think of this:

After that winter, I would never be the same again.

Does that sound convincing to you?

Triumph

No one believes in anything much anymore—though a few of the passionately intense will press the case for implanting microchips in immigrants—but as recently as twenty years ago, Triumph was a major theme in American movies.

The movies were invariably about sports. There was Triumph in war as well, but all the death made that Triumph less thematically pure, so sports was the go-to. The sports movies dealt with an underdog who won. That was it. That was the whole movie. It was at the very end that the underdog won, against impossible odds and after suffering setbacks, and the last shot was a freeze-frame of the underdog aloft. If it was a movie about a solo sport, the winner was captured jumping in the air pumping his (it was usually a guy) fists; if a team sport, the frozen image was of the most valuable player hoisted onto his teammates' shoulders, brandishing a trophy. That freeze-frame was about all there was of honesty in those movies because, in real life, after Triumph, everything does come to a dead halt. Sometimes it's death by violent burnout, more often the slow ooze of élan vital. If you don't believe me, try asking anyone who's ever landed on the moon what it was like returning to Davenport, Iowa, and the Rotarians. "It wasn't the same" will be the reply.

For a cautionary tale about the career of Triumph, I think ruefully of Edward VIII and Wallis Warfield Simpson—not often, but for the purposes of argument. Edward loved the twice-divorced Wallis so much that he abdicated the throne for her, setting in motion a constitutional crisis. Their love was the great romantic frisson of the twentieth century, even if Edward's epicene manner spurred rumors that he was homosexual and many still insist that Wallis was genetically male—so maybe it did work out for them after all; but I digress. The point is what happened after. Edward lost a realm and embarked with his wife on a shallow, meaningless, peripatetic existence. They were pensioned off—it was a substantial pension— and wandered aimlessly among England's colonial possessions and, increasingly, former colonial possessions. All they ever did was smoke and drink tea and spirits while seated in wicker chairs next to trees with very large fronds. They weren't welcome on the British mainland, whatever that was, or even in Scotland, and at times it seemed the only person willing to speak to them was Noël Coward. Now, if only one person is willing to speak to you, you could

do worse than Noël Coward. He was the wittiest Englishman of his time and a rabid suck-up to any royal, or semi-
deposed royal, who crossed his path. He had started out as
an enfant terrible in the twenties writing scandalous plays
about young cocaine addicts with Oedipus complexes, and
went on to give us two or three of the greatest stage comedies of the twentieth century, but all that paled beside the
success he enjoyed as a stunningly gifted bounder. Noël
Coward wrote a novel called *Pomp and Circumstance* that
is exactly as reprehensible as it is delightful, and it is totally
delightful. It's set in a fictional island colony where the
childlike and scantily clad natives have the good sense to
loooove being subjects of the Crown. This is because their
pukka sahib masters (that's India, actually) take care of all
the paperwork, freeing up the natives to spend all day doing
whatever it is they do all day. I forget. I think they may take
a page from Margaret Mead's Samoans and have nonstop
guiltless, lyrical sex. This really doesn't matter. My point is
that while Edward and Wallis, by then styled the Duke and
Duchess of Windsor, bickered a lot and drank a lot and
weren't allowed to talk to their family and pretty much
lived like the Flying Dutchman on an expense account, at
least they had Noël Coward to talk to. And yet—Edward
had been king!

I once saw a documentary about the daily lives of the
royal family. It turns out they spend most of their time
traveling to strip malls, where they shake hands with

minimum-wage workers in stretch pants. That's the queen. Lesser royals are forced to meet up with the senile potentates of former possessions to whom, in the spirit of chummy nostalgia, they say things like "I gave you your freedom." Maybe you're better off sharing sundowners with Noël Coward. That's not for me to say.

My *point* is, stories of Triumph are very sad stories and only the mercy of the freeze-frame saves us from knowing this.

A Plea for Universal Misunderstanding

Not long ago, I was on a panel devoted to discussion of a show I was working on.

The show took place in The Past.

Inevitably, the question arose as to how this period story was relevant to Our Present Moment.

I always zone out when this is the issue, but dimly I heard my copanelists sweetly contorting themselves to explain how, Yes, Though the Show Seemed to Be About The Past, the Very Same Conditions Prevail to This Very Day. Indeed, Similar Things Are Happening All the Time. Why, Just Last Week in Tierra del Fuego . . .

It's not the question itself I find irksome, but the assumptions that underlie it.

Why must all stories be versions of our own?

Why, to hold our interest, does every story have to reflect what we think we know about ourselves?

Are we worried about what might happen if we attended

to something else? Do we fear the culture suffers from a shortage of mirrors?

Do we really *believe* all stories are at bottom the same story? Is that a useful insight? Has it proved handy in our global entanglements?

At the cellular level, we're all very much alike. Once there's further differentiation, we—how shall I put this?—differ.

When Demi Moore got her hands on *The Scarlet Letter*, Hester Prynne was given a happy ending because We Know So Much More Now Than They Did Back Then.

This is the degradation of empathy.

I'd like to see a production of *Coriolanus* in which Coriolanus is not Benito Mussolini but is Coriolanus and it's just weird.

Real enlightenment will come when we find ourselves saying, "My God, I don't get this at all."

Presence

In 2008, I feared for the future of making an entrance.

I was in rehearsal for a play that featured a number of youngish people—people in their late twenties or just beyond. One day, I got there early. Because I liked the members of this company, I was looking forward to greeting them as they showed up. Only they never did show up. Each wafted into the room hooked to a device. This was early days for texting and its hushed rites were still unfamiliar to me. No one spoke. Technically, everyone was present and accounted for, yet there was no question of violating their separate communions. They struck me as devout yet bland. I felt as though I were at a funeral for someone who in life had not been hated and in death was not mourned. When, at different rates, the actors emerged to acknowledge the room that, after all, had been their destination, it was too late for hellos, and even if it hadn't been, they were in no mood. They were exactly like babies waking from an untroubled nap: milky, dreamy-eyed, pleased to see you but not yet ready to play. This was not what I was used to. I had long had an idea of arrival. It was an autumnal thing—rustling, crackling-nerved; eager, full persons entering on a gust of information. Here and Elsewhere were sharply delineated spaces, and Here, when rent by the knife thrust of a new person, would come alive with news of Elsewhere. Eons ago, the legendary stage actress Eva Le Gallienne lamented what she saw as a lack of "attack" among younger actors. In 2008, I understood what she was talking about. How can people who don't enter rooms possibly enter plays?

Fittingly, the best entrance I ever saw an actor make captured this quality of elsewhereness. The actor was Talia Balsam and she was in a very charming ten-minute play by Craig Lucas. Her role was that of someone expected at an art gallery. Because she was half a generation older than the kids in my play, we first saw her *talking* on her cell phone, not texting on it, and, also unlike them, she was, in her absence, ferociously present. The phone call obviously rankled, something about it made her irate, and it was the full, scabrous force of her personality she sent off into the ether. I had never before seen someone enter a play so in the middle of things. She had not simply vaulted onstage from the dark, neutral vestibule of offstage. Her engagement configured the space she was coming from and let us know that, like the space she had just wandered into, it was inessential. Places were now unreal; they'd been vanquished by our ability to send instant signals to other unreal places. I'd never before thought much about how actors got themselves onstage and I don't retrospectively judge against those other entrances. What made Talia Balsam's entrance so special was not that it was incredibly well executed, though it was, but that it was defining. This is how we enter now, it declared: on a technicality. "Here" is not the place it used to be and, having been wised up to this, I wondered why people paid so much attention to their bodies. (Selfies weren't popular yet.)

Anecdote

Kathleen Turner once stole a cab from me.

This was in the nineties. It was a blustery afternoon and I was standing on the corner of Broadway and Seventy-Sixth Street. I'd snagged a cab—it was pulling up—when I heard a voice behind me say, "That's *mine.*"

I turned and beheld.

She was already middle-aged and she was a stunning woman. I'd recognized her by her voice before I'd even turned around—it was that slightly slurred, somewhat Southern, honey-coated wondrousness, a half octave up from where it lives now.

"I'm c-o-o-o-ld!" Kathleen Turner said.

And to help me understand the concept of "cold," she hugged herself and whinnied a little.

I had no problem with this. You can always find a taxi on Broadway in the seventies.

Besides, all Kathleen Turner got out of the deal was a cab; I had an anecdote.

[HEALTH, EDUCATION]

Goodness

I used to be good, then I started getting bronchitis.

These were violent sieges, sometimes lasting six months and leading to a general systemic weakening, favorable to ancillary debilities.

Partial deafness, arrhythmia, tooth decay; the list was long.

Wracked, I was no longer in fettle to be good. I didn't attend friends' events or children's birthday parties. I didn't do more than my share or even my share. Instead, I lay on the sofa, which is now concave.

Once goodness was out of the question, I aimed to be unoffending. It turned out that to be unoffending while not showing up for anything required copious explanation of my condition—in other words, a plethora of me—so that in the effort not to *offend*, I *exhausted*.

These days, I strive to be *droll* yet *invisible*.

Doctors/Diagnosticians

Last March, kittens moved into my chest.

They came singly at first, mewing pathetically, a lonely keening noise, as if they'd been buffeted by a weather event and were crying to be brought home. They came mostly at night when I was trying to get to sleep. Sometimes they kept me up and sometimes they woke me up.

After a while, the solitary kittens were joined by other kittens, their enemies, and the two sides engaged in alley-style brawls. I would try regulating my breathing to prove that the kittens weren't kittens at all, merely a respiratory side effect. It changed nothing. The kittens were true and proud kittens, squatting in my chest and contemptuous of my rights as their bodily overlord. For months I did nothing to address the situation because for months I do nothing to address any situation. Then I was set to spend two nights in upstate New York, where they have many allergens, and I made an appointment to see my doctor. I suspected that what I had was asthma, and I kept picturing myself thrashing on a rustic hotel bed, unable to breathe and without a rescue inhaler. It made sense that I'd have asthma because I'd had Hodgkin's disease and, according to Doug, who is a playwright, asthma often follows Hodgkin's. True, that had been twenty years ago, which sounded like kind of a long latency period, but what was I, a doctor?

Dr. Miller listened to my chest and told me definitively that I didn't have asthma, so I asked him about my second choice: lung cancer. This also seemed reasonable; odor trespass works oddly in my building and some nights in my bedroom I could tell that one of my neighbors smokes.

He said I didn't have lung cancer, either, and as is often the case when I've been declared free of mortal disease, I didn't press for further information and Dr. Miller, more cautious than intrusive, let me leave without a protocol.

Over the next few weeks, the kittens grew into cats and their skirmishes worsened. Meanwhile, I had a recurrence of sciatica. The two conditions together started to feel possibly intolerable and I decided I should choose one and really go proactive on it. Sciatica always went away on its own, so I picked the cats and made an appointment, this time with my cardiologist. Though I didn't think the problem was actually heart related, I hadn't seen my cardiologist in a long time, and the cats were in my chest so at least it was his vicinity.

When I got there, I told him I couldn't have an EKG because if I had to lie on a table with my sciatica, I'd scream, and I didn't want to demoralize the waiting room. He asked if I was certain that it *was* sciatica. I assured him that I was because, though the last time it had presented in my buttock and was now in my coccyx, according to my friend Joanne, a casting director, the sciatic is the longest nerve in the body, which renders the entire region vulnerable.

Dr. Timoney seconded Jane's opinion and arranged with his nurse to perform a stand-up EKG, which I had never heard of and which hurt only a little. The results were normal, as had been the results of all the other tests he'd done, and he told me it sounded as though I had acid reflux, which surprised me, because I didn't have heartburn. All my doctors are in the same building—I'm looking to get a pied-à-terre there—and while I dressed, Dr. Timoney called Dr. Miller for a consult. When he came back, he told me that Dr. Miller had listened to my list of symptoms, said, "Do you think it could be acid reflux?" and prescribed Prilosec.

I took the Prilosec diligently for three weeks. It helped a little, then plateaued.

When I called my actress friend Patti to ask her advice about this, she said I was going to develop esophageal cancer, and hung up.

Later, my friend Randi, who's a singer, phoned. I told her about the reflux, and she said I had to *stop* the Prilosec, which actually *causes* reflux, and instead eat a small quantity of sea salt once an hour. Also, I needed to take a wonderful product called Performer's Magic, which would cure my hoarseness. I did both but stuck with the Prilosec, too, as a sort of backup. Again, things got a little better, then leveled off.

Two days later, my sister-in-law called to tell me about the new pillows on her home furnishings website. She ordered me to get a massage for the sciatica, which I would never do, and was outraged, simply outraged, when I told her about the Prilosec.

"*Prilosec*?" she cried. "Why not *Zantac*? It's so much better."

I told her that Prilosec had been prescribed by my doctor, who is a G.I. and a distinguished one, and she asked if I'd had an endoscopy. I said I hadn't, and she was outraged for the second time in one phone call.

"Your brother and I have them *yearly*."

Then she said that their wonderful friend Mitchell, who had had regular colonoscopies, never had an endoscopy and now was dead two years from stomach cancer. I promised her I would get an endoscopy when my schedule lifted a little.

That afternoon, Leslie phoned me. She herself had been plagued by gastric problems lately, nausea and diarrhea, and on my recommendation had gone to see Dr. Miller, who diagnosed a parasite, though the women in her psychodrama group thought it might be candida.

I asked her if she'd ever had an endoscopy. She said she hadn't so I told her about Mitchell's stomach cancer. She started to panic and I said, "For Christ's sake, Leslie, that doesn't mean *you're* going to get it, too," in an effort to bully her back into the wits I'd scared her out of.

Over the next three weeks, the cats added recruits and I think opened a second front. Randi came for lunch, and when I showed her the salt I was taking, which was the brand she'd recommended, she told me that while it was the right *brand* it was the wrong *kind*—the crystals were too big, they'd never melt on my tongue—and asked if I was still taking Performer's Magic. I told her I was, sometimes, and it helped a little.

The sciatica got a bit better and I had a reading of a play with Linda Lavin, whom I hadn't seen in seventeen years. She commanded me to give up tomatoes and citrus fruit and make an appointment to see Dr. Weissman, who is Top Dog in the reflux game. I told her that Randi had recommended Performer's Magic. Linda saw Randi and raised her, saying that Dr. Weissman had *invented* Performer's Magic. Then she instructed me not to mind that he had been sued for malpractice by a knight.

The next afternoon, I visited my father at his assisted-living facility. His usual aide, Angela, had the day off. Her substitute, Michelle, a pleasant Bahamian lady, declared that the one true cure for reflux was to drink eucalyptus drops dissolved in a small amount of tepid water. When the drops came from Amazon, the label on the bottle said Not For Internal Use. I was ambivalent, then decided not to take them. The next day when, in the spirit of self-deprecation, I shared this story with Ruth, my Peruvian cleaning lady, she laughed only a little, then confided her belief that I didn't have reflux at all, this was just another attack of the bronchitis that I'm prone to. She prescribed a mixture of green tea, honey, and watercress. That was the elixir used by everyone in her country, and they all had beautiful lungs and bronchia, though sometimes they died prematurely in contract hits ordered by wealthy men who bribed the authorities not to arrest them.

The tea tasted weird and did no good. However, the sciatica went away completely, and to celebrate, I scheduled an endoscopy, which I had to cancel when a terrible throbbing started in my upper gum. I arranged an emergency appointment with my dentist. When I got there, I told Veronica, the receptionist, that my upper left wisdom tooth was badly impacted. She shuffled me into the X-ray room and when the X-rays were developed came in and said, "What are you now, a dentist?"

"Why?" I asked.

"You have a badly impacted upper left wisdom tooth."

"I know," I said. "I told you that."

Sleep

It's wonderful how redemptive a change in category can be. For instance, I used to be an insomniac. Insomnia is a pathology associated with a wide array of negative health outcomes. Recently, I learned that I can, if I choose, stop being an insomniac and become instead a "segmented sleeper." It turns out the folk wisdom that we require eight consecutive unconscious hours is balderdash. Sleeping in spurts is every bit as restorative. I can't tell you how happy that makes me. Now I am a committed practitioner of segmented sleep. Here's how it goes:

I'm writing this on a Thursday. On Tuesday, I had a sleep segment that ran from roughly 2:45 a.m. through 3:34 a.m. My next sleep segment came on Wednesday, starting at about 3:07 a.m. and concluding at 4:28 a.m. Monday, I didn't do as well, but I'm new at this.

Oddly, I'm not finding my segmented sleep much more refreshing than my insomnia was. I expect this is a psychological hangover from my insomniac days and will ebb as I gain experience. One of the advantages of segmented sleep is that, barring early appointments, you can force yourself to have it. What I mean is, when I was an insomniac, I was a defeatist, who at a certain hour would just throw in the towel. As a segmented sleeper, I will stay in bed until noon if I have to, to nab that one last segment of sleep. This works surprisingly well.

There are the dreams, of course. Second, or subsequent, sleep has a different quality from first sleep. I haven't consulted a specialist about this, but I'm willing to bet that it isn't deep-REM (rapid eye movement) sleep but something more along the lines of shallow-PHLEGM (phlegmatic eye movement) sleep. The dreams that come in this later sleep are disturbing. Not precisely nightmares, they're naturalistic in an off way, and you always remember them when you wake up. Your dead friends and relatives appear, and they're annoying. Often, there's a big-box store. In this past week, I've been dreaming a lot about food, which raises the question: Am I hungry? Last night, I dreamt that, as a punishment for something, I had to stock miles of bookshelves with my books, which I numbered with a magic marker: one to five million. Suddenly I was a bridegroom and the wedding march had five million steps, only it was the wedding *rehearsal*, not the ceremony, and at the dinner there was the issue of not spilling food on the clothes, which were the wedding clothes. This meant I had to refrain from eating, though the food looked succulent, in a heavily sauced way. Again: hungry? Supposedly, when you dream about a wedding it means death, but . . . somebody else's, right?

Whatever kinks still need to be ironed out, I'm very grateful to be a segmented sleeper, and now, if you'll excuse me, I'm going to take advantage of the recent discovery that eating salt is actually good for us.

Oblivion

Once, I underwent a procedure for my heart.

As I lay on the slab being anesthetized, I had no inkling of God but was pierced by an exquisite understanding of Michael Jackson.

I had never given much thought to Michael Jackson beyond the casual, "Oh. Wow. Strange." Nor was I especially susceptible to his (I'm told) undeniable genius as a performer, so this was not a communion I was expecting.

But the drug they were dosing me with was propofol, the very drug that killed the King of Pop, and therein lay our merger of souls.

This is what propofol does not do:

It does not supply you with some swift and vanishing orgasmic rush after which you feel all cheap and used.

Instead, propofol draws you into the plushest oblivion imaginable—unimaginable, really. It wipes away all terror of Last Things, of physical extremity and Hell, wooing, easing, consuming you. It is the dream of a lovely death.

A doctor employed propofol to put Michael Jackson to sleep every night, and I am here to tell you that, given the money and upper-echelon/back-street connections, anybody in his proper, quaking mind would hire a doctor to do the same for him. Perhaps a less distracted doctor.

Perhaps not.

One thing is certain: Michael Jackson died a happy man.

Malpractice

One of the great serendipitous pleasures of life is achieving a desired end by telling the truth. I'm basically unfamiliar with the phenomenon and the few times it's happened to me, I've felt embarrassed, sort of exposed and uneasy, and once or twice I've cried. Mostly, when I want something, I shape the truth. I place a strong emphasis on what may be a secondary aspect of the situation, at best.

I'm far from alone in this. My friend Kat regularly calls me up to try out her alibis, even though, often, no alibi is needed. One time she had to get out of participating in a reading shortly before the reading was scheduled to happen. "I'm going to say that they're about to foreclose on my sister's house," she told me, "unless I guarantee her loan, in person, at the lawyers' that afternoon." The truth was she was having a tonsillectomy. I suggested that if she wanted to let them know about the tonsillectomy, it would probably play. She went with the foreclosed sister. I understood completely.

This is why, during voir dire the other day, when we were asked if we might have a bias in the case that was being tried, I felt all lofty and patriotic that, before I could even tell it to, my arm shot up. A truth-telling arm it was that morning.

The subject of the suit was medical malpractice.

I have excellent doctors now, lots and lots of excellent doctors, but I cannot tell you how many times I have been medically malpracticed upon. One of my recurring dreams is that I'm one of those sallow, impoverished people who support themselves by selling their blood and participating in that kind of study where you're required to sign a form absolving the testers of responsibility in your near-certain death. I'm not going to go into too much detail about what's been done to me because it's pretty dreary but—Jesus!

A lot of it happened when I had this diagnosis-defying condition that landed me in the hospital for two months. The doctors ordered every test known to man. One morning I was relieved of fourteen vials of blood and a nurse let me know that the lab had developed a grudge against me because some nights the techs were kept there just to run my results. One doctor claimed I was a "fascinoma." This is a medical term. It means "I got my degree in Guadalajara." Really, they couldn't figure me out.

One of the tests involved shoving something up my rectum. The doctor running it declined to give me anesthesia and promised that he would shove the thing only so far and it would not be far enough to hurt. Actually, it hurt a good deal. I pointed this out to him when the exam was over. "I went farther than I'd planned to," he told me. "Why?" I said. "Because you didn't ask me to stop," he explained.

After I was better, the receptionist from that doctor's office called to let me know, shyly, and laughing a little, that my payment for their services was five dollars under. Would I send a check for the five? "Of course," I reassured her. Obviously, there was no way I was sending that check. When she called again to ask after it, this time not so sweetly, I recounted the story of the doctor's anal molestation of me, complete with his verbatim quote. "So here's your option: you can have the five bucks plus a malpractice suit or we can forget the whole thing." I never heard from them again.

Finally it was determined that I had Hodgkin's disease. This was presented to me as good news. "It's Hodgkin's and we're gonna cure it," somebody said. As I'm the only member of my demographic without advanced medical training, I accepted this and never asked a question.

A year later, Jacqueline Onassis died of non-Hodgkin's lymphoma and in *People* magazine there was a side-by-side comparison of the symptoms of non-Hodgkin's and Hodgkin's. It turned out I was textbook. I had no symptoms that weren't symptoms of Hodgkin's. I decided that next time some doctor called me a "fascinoma," I was going to ditch that doctor and refer my case directly to the editors of *People* magazine. It would save a lot of time.

Another funny thing. Twenty years later, I asked my oncologist why, at the end of every checkup, he said he was "proud" of me. After all, I'd only had Hodgkin's, which has a fantastic recovery rate, and except for certain skin cancers, is the cancer to get if you have to get cancer.

"But yours was *very far along* when we caught it," he said.

"It was?"

"You knew that."

Nope. Didn't. No one had ever bothered to mention it.

Despite all this, during the private portion of my voir-dire interview, I wasn't really thinking of myself. I was thinking of any number of my friends, and I was becoming aware that as I was speaking, I was growing redder and redder and my voice was tightening and getting shrill and it dawned on me that this was not the demeanor you wanted to present in a public building in the post-9/11 era. It's just that my friends have been so badly served.

A number of them have been in therapy, and one way or another they've all been screwed by it.

There was Isabella, who swore by her shrink even after that shrink was sent to prison on an extortion rap.

And, of course, Emma, whose relationship with her shrink got so tormented, they went into couples counseling together.

She went into couples counseling with her shrink.

Emma, at least, finally left that shrink. She became instantly happy when she did. Not since I was nine and my parents informed me that I would not have to return the following summer to Camp Monchatea had anyone been so rapidly released into glowing mental health.

Nevertheless, it was Emma who was on my mind as I colored in that voir-dire interview.

Emma is a professional with a very fancy job at a famous arts institution, and she is impeccable at it. If she has a flaw, and she probably does, it's that she has trouble delegating responsibility. This is because she equates errors with sins and does not believe that sins can be venial. She's getting better at this since she's given up therapy—still, it's her personality. The thing about people like Emma is that they live for those moments when they can cede control. In Emma's case, this happens chiefly at the doctor's office.

Emma's main doctor was a woman named Judith Abravanel. Dr. Abravanel had a wall full of diplomas from the Ivy League and a warm, enveloping gaze. Emma does the work she does mostly because there was a program in it at an Ivy League university, and after sullenly accepting her BA from a state school, she would have pursued a graduate degree in almost any program the Ivy League saw fit to offer her. The wall of diplomas would have been enough as far as Emma was concerned; throw in that seductive gaze and she was a goner. She worshipped Dr. Abravanel even though over the years, she'd had to repeat herself often enough that she'd begun to suspect that behind that gaze, what the doctor was really thinking was, "What if I added cumin to the marinade?"

The other thing that distinguished Dr. Abravanel was her Theory.

She had published a number of articles about a segment of the doctor-going population she referred to as the Haunted Healthy.

You could pore over these articles with the aid of a fine-toothed comb and the full active membership of the AMA without gleaning how the Haunted Healthy differ in a single particular from your garden variety hypochondriac. That didn't matter to the good doctor. She'd trademarked the phrase.

Over the course of her practice Dr. Abravanel had noted a curious phenomenon: a number of her patients insisted they were ill when—this will astonish you—they were actually healthy!

She must have had nine or ten patients who had exhibited this trait.

Had she been a woman of science, Dr. Abravanel might have dismissed the findings from a sampling this size as anecdotal, but for her, nine was plenty.

And once she'd trademarked the Haunted Healthy, she began to find them everywhere.

A patient of Dr. Abravanel had something like a sixty-five percent chance of not *being* sick, just *thinking* she was sick.

This suited Emma fine. Like me, she is something of a hypochondriac, and hypochondria is a technique for reassuring yourself that you're impervious to illness. Your symptoms keep meaning nothing.

Things got a little hairy only when Emma started falling in the street.

She would be walking to work when—thwack!—face-plant.

This was disconcerting. She wasn't blacking out—at least, she didn't think she was—but she was falling. In public. Before the good burghers of the Upper West Side.

She worried about her legs, about Parkinson's, about Lou Gehrig's disease.

"Psychosomatic!" decreed Dr. Abravanel in her Field Marshal voice.

This didn't sound right to Emma. It didn't *feel* right to her. Nevertheless, she trusted her doctor implicitly, and Dr. Abravanel had that gift common to charismatics, world leaders, and demagogues—the ability to estrange people from their perceptions.

What should she do about the falling, though?

"Relax!"

Emma tried relaxing. She went to the gym. She

scheduled a weekly mani-pedi. She fell and fell. Why did this keep happening? she asked the doctor.

"Stress!"

This sounded plausible to Emma. How should she relieve her stress?

"Go to the gym!"

Emma explained that she already went to the gym.

"Have a mani-pedi!"

"I do that, too," said Emma.

"Sex!"

"I find that sex increases stress."

Dr. Abravanel took Emma's hand. "Oh, Emma, Emma," she said, hauled out her warm, enveloping gaze, and spoke no more that day.

Emma fell and fell and fell and fell and found Dr. Abravanel's suggestions less and less practicable. ("The Poconos!") She asked about getting an MRI.

"Absolutely *not*," said the doctor.

"But—"

The doctor pulled out the big guns.

"What's *haunting* you, Emma?"

"I don't like falling in the street."

"Well," chortled the doctor, "at least you're short." She was really quite merry about the whole situation.

In the end, what saved Emma was her nineteenth-century outlook. She more than believed in respectability;

it was the pap of life to her. All this falling on the street! There was the whiff of vagrancy about it. Finally, she insisted Dr. Abravanel refer her to a neurologist.

Indulgently, the doctor said, "There, there, little one. Well, as long as you're doing this unnecessary thing, go with the best. I'll set you up with Dr. Massimo Fortelli."

At the moment, Dr. Fortelli was visiting his family in Modena. He would be back in March. This was January.

In February, when Emma could no longer stand up without keeling over, she checked herself into St. Luke's–Roosevelt Hospital. There, the genuinely warm and brilliant neurologist assigned to her discovered she had a brain tumor the size of a Spalding ball. Emma's head is the size of a cantaloupe. She underwent surgery the next day and, except for one post-op seizure, has been well ever since. Had she followed Dr. Abravanel's orders and waited for Dr. Fortelli, she'd be dead.

Though Emma's friends begged her to sue Dr. Abravanel, when you're on the other side of a crisis so shaking, you really have no stomach for that sort of thing.

And I'm such a nice guy I don't even hope that one day soon Dr. Abravanel will misdiagnose herself as "haunted" and die excruciatingly from a tumor the size of a bowling ball. Really, I can't even conceive of such a thing on the level of fantasy.

I am comforted, though, by the idea that that doctor

whose case I was excused from—whoever that doctor is and whatever that doctor did—might right now be rotting away in a prison cell, license stripped, and every last asset sold off to cover damages.

What a nice thought that is. You should see me thinking it. You'd get lost in my warm, enveloping gaze.

Age

Two times this week, people sent me e-mails containing suggestions that were not feasible.

I answered them at length, patiently explaining why it was impossible for me to do what they advised.

Each of them replied, "Actually, I was joking."

You need to know this was not a generational thing. One of my correspondents was my age, the other fourteen years older. The problem wasn't that I don't know what "on fleek" means or something like that. (As it happens, I do know what "on fleek" means.)

It wasn't a question of relative age, but of absolute age.

I am growing old. I'm turning into someone who doesn't get the joke.

CITY FRIENDS,
NEW AND UPDATED

Deferred

I pride myself on my dread because I consider it so much more intelligent than free-floating anxiety—dread has real-world correlatives and can be justified, while free-floating anxiety suggests weak character—but while my dread is often a source of pride, it's never a source of pleasure. I was deep in dread last week, during the wee small hours, and it possessed all the standard attributes—white knuckles, clammy skin, shortness of breath. Despite this, it's possible I was being a little bit of a phony. The dread might well have been born as free-floating anxiety, which, because I had such contempt for it, I strove to recast as dread and so found an object to attach it to. Either way, the feeling was real and rattling, and though I took steps to exorcise it and those steps were, superficially, successful, I'm not convinced the situation has been rectified. This calm might be a false calm. The dread might reach up out of its grave at any moment and grab at me, like that hand at the end of *Carrie*.

The source of my dread—or its trumped-up object—was my friend who dreams of murder. Or, perhaps, dreamed of murder.

Because the object of his homicidal daydreams has died.

I was circumspect about the following fact when he was alive, but now I feel free to tell you that the nemesis was my friend's father; I don't think this will come as much of a surprise.

My homicidal friend had always hated his father, and his father, whom I knew a little, was, quite frankly, hateful. There'd been a quiescent passage when, like most very old people, he had, by dint of enfeeblement, subsided into the human condition and become less offensive. That passed. Soon enough, he was as sour and bullying as ever, and my friend found himself toiling sweatily and in vain to persuade new people passing through his father's life— sympathetic health care workers and the like—that this awfulness was his lifelong personality and not merely the disinhibited side effects of great age.

When it happened, my friend sent me this e-mail:

Dad just croaked. Diner?

I wrote back:

Tomorrow 10 a.m. Condolences?????

I didn't know what to expect from him, but if pressed, I'd have bet on a gala mood. You never know, though. He might have come on like Michael O'Keefe in *The Great Santini*, who, when his despised father died as he'd always prayed he would, sobbed his way to an Oscar nomination confessing the horrified suspicion that his father had "run into one of those prayers." In a similar situation, this would probably be my response. But then, I manufacture guilt with such efficiency you'd think I had a loom.

What surprised me was that my murderous friend still seemed murderous.

It's sentimental of us to expect that large events will wring instantaneous changes. Even so, I'd thought he might at least exhibit a different shade in his long-narrowed spectrum. No such luck.

"How are you?" I asked warily.

I believe you would describe the look he gave me as "gimlet-eyed."

"Talk."

"My father died."

"And . . . you belatedly realize you *loved* him?"

"Who *are* you?"

"I keep my mind open to all possibilities."

"A mind is a terrible thing to open."

"Then what?"

"He *died* in his *sleep*."

"So?"

"It was painless, and on his face there was a tranquil expression."

I think I've mentioned that my friend has an imposing voice. He went through the acting program at Juilliard, where they are notorious for their resonance, and the upshot of his training is that he doesn't have to do anything extraordinary for his voice to become the dominant fact in a room. I could see people listening and, as usual when people listen to my friend, what he was saying was shocking.

"My father died peacefully when he deserved to die in agony!"

In an unrelated incident, a waiter dropped a dish.

"Would you please *lower your voice*?" I'd never said that before.

"My voice already is low. It just happens to be beautiful."

"Listen. So he died peacefully, so what?"

"Is there no justice in the world?" he phonated.

"You know there isn't."

"Every time I did something nice for him, I was betraying my mother."

This is the sentence that will be carved on his tombstone. My friend loved his mother as much as he hated his father. The love and hatred existed in a fixed relationship, like a law of mechanics.

"You did *not* betray your mother. You were *lovely* to your mother."

"When she was *alive*. Once she died, I was supposed to avenge her."

Sometimes you'll see an actor in a porn movie and wonder if his enormous penis gave him the idea to go into porn or if he'd always intended to go into porn and he just happened to grow an enormous penis. I ask myself a similar question about my friend's thunderous voice and his penchant for melodramatic utterance.

"We are not avengers," I said. "We're New Yorkers."

He was almost trembling by then, and defensive glibness was not going to improve the situation. I decided to give banality another try.

"This feeling will pass."

"You don't understand," he said. And he said it in a normal-person whisper.

I do understand, actually.

His father's meanness had been indiscriminate, but he deployed it with a sniper's precision when it came to his wife. It was as though he had married her to beat her down. I've always suspected there was some event at the root of this, some early expression of sexual repulsion to which this vicious behavior was a kind of rebuttal—my friend is an only child. That doesn't excuse it.

In spastic style yet miraculously, when the couple were in their early seventies, they divorced. No one could track the steps or credit it. My friend's mom had finally had enough, and his dad, grunting something like "Good riddance," went along.

It was a strange, jangled time for the mom. She was in the rapture of freedom and didn't know how she felt about it. She had enough money—my friend had to superintend the money—and she'd kept the country club membership in the divorce, so there was something of a sodality, but her days felt weightless and time often turned against her. Sometimes she missed her marriage, even the daily savagery of it. At other times, the exhilaration frightened her—she was *too* buoyant, she didn't recognize herself, and she felt that giddiness-unto-nausea that's like the feeling you get under gas.

There were highlights. After an evening of mah jong at the Club, she reported to my friend her outrage—delicious outrage—at the treatment she'd received from some of the men there. She was a beautiful woman still, and, unmarried, had become catnip to the over-seventy set. "Some of them are my friends' husbands!" she cried. Oh, what a time she'd had!

She'd managed to bank one good month—one month when she could envision happiness as a feature of her routine—before the diagnosis came down: stage IV breast cancer. This was when my friend's filial devotion entered its activist phase. He squired her to treatment, held her hand, stayed overnight, partnered her in cards, listened,

listened, listened. His father never called her, and when my friend, dutiful beyond his own interests, called his father, the old man never mentioned the cancer, except once, to say, "So the bitch is sick."

His mother didn't die immediately, and there was the odd good day. She was not one of those prodigies you hear about who go into glorious remissions that linger and extend and suddenly no trace of cancer is detectable. She worsened and was moved to the hospital, where she was palliated, fell into a coma, then stayed that way.

One day after my friend had been at her bedside for seventeen hours straight—he hadn't even bathed, and he's a fastidious man—a doctor said, "You should go home. It's not going to be today."

Hungry and aching for a shower, he trusted the doctor and hailed a cab.

Here I'm going to say a few words about the Bloomberg administration. It will only *feel* like a digression.

Mayor Michael Bloomberg was famous for a number of qualities, chief among them his ungodly wealth. When there was a shortfall in the city's budget, he'd cover it by writing a check, and when he decided he'd like to serve a third term, which was illegal, he bought a new law.

Prominent among the things he's known for that were *not* (on the face of it) related to money was one of his major staff appointments, that of Janette Sadik-Khan.

Janette Sadik-Khan was Bloomberg's traffic tsar. In

this capacity, she wielded a management style that, had she been a man, would have led to her being called a "dynamo." As a woman, she enjoyed other sobriquets.

The first fact Janette Sadik-Khan needed to have known by everyone, particularly underlings and negotiating partners, was that she was *right*. At all times and about all things.

What made this especially galling was that, by and large, she was right about her rightness.

Under her rule, pollution diminished and safety increased. Times Square, once a hideously ugly snarl of cars and trucks, wondrously transformed into a hideously ugly pedestrian plaza.

And, if you believed statistics, vehicular traffic flowed more smoothly than ever.

Nobody believes statistics. To those benighted among us who still made their passage through the city chiefly via automobile, traffic was the worst it had ever been.

Because of the bicycles.

Major roadways now featured dedicated bicycle lanes, square footage of turf that had been taken—purloined! plundered!—from the cars and trucks to which it rightfully belonged. In the beginning, these lanes appeared to be lightly used. This meant that yards of precious pavement had been repurposed for no reason at all. Now when you were stuck in traffic, it was the result of sheer human arrogance. (Before the bicycles, any traffic you'd been stuck in had been an act of God.)

In short order, Janette Sadik-Khan found herself installed as one of the city's favorite villains. Cindy Adams, the noted urbanist, and a cherished New York gossip columnist since 1857, demonized her with puns, and others followed suit. She was Krazy Khan! Janette the Sadistic Khan Artist!

And not only because of the bicycles.

Perhaps even more loathed was her prohibition of the left turn.

In the borough of Manhattan, you were no longer allowed to make a left turn into any intersection where you'd really like to. No one understood why. The rule screwed everything up. Trips that once took ten minutes now took ninety. Throw in rush hour and you might as well just book a room. I get that this is a white person's problem. The population of Darfur would *kill* to be caught in a New York City traffic jam. For my friend, though, it had a very sad consequence.

At his mother's bedside the day the doctor sent him home, he had lost all sense of time. It's amazing he caught a cab, really, because it was the witching hour and, even before the reign of the visionary Sadik-Khan, you didn't want to know from that. My friend didn't mind so much. He was exhausted and had almost fallen asleep—probably he *had* fallen asleep—when his cell phone emitted the opening phrases of Fauré's "Élégie." It was the hospital.

"You'd better get here. Your mom's taken a turn. She's going fast."

"Oh God."

"But she woke up. She's asking for you."

My friend looked around him. Somehow, the cab was in traffic, he had no idea when that had happened. They were about two miles from the hospital, moving slowly, but moving. He rapped his knuckles against the plexiglass security divider.

"We have to go back!"

The cabbie didn't get it. "You want to get out?"

"No. To the hospital. You have to take me back to the hospital."

"You want me to pull over?"

"TAKE ME BACK TO THE FUCKING HOSPITAL, YOU GODDAMNED IDIOT!!"

"You want to go back to the hospital?"

". . . Yes!"

"Oh. Okay."

The car just kept going as it was.

"What the fuck are you doing?" asked my friend.

"You want to go back to the hospital?"

"Yes."

"I'm *taking* you back to the hospital."

"Why are you still going in this direction?"

"Sir, what do you want me to do?"

"TAKE ME BACK TO THE FUCKING HOSPITAL!"

"I'M TAKING YOU BACK TO THE FUCKING HOSPITAL!"

"You need to make a left!"

"No left turn."

"You have to make a left turn."

"No, sir. No left turn for twenty blocks."

"My mother is dying, *turn left!*"

"Two citations, sir. One more, they take away my medallion."

"YOU GODDAMN MORON, MAKE A LEFT!"

"Sir, you *want* another cab? *Take* another cab."

"I don't want another cab—*what* other cab?—you just have to turn around."

"No left turn."

By now my friend's body had turned against him. It was seething, overheating, he had to cool it down. Unconsciously, he had begun to pull at his clothing.

"Listen—do you have no compassion? My *mother—*"

"No left turn, sir. Medallion."

The heat was unbearable, he was trembling, it was like the DTs. He had to master his body, shuck off the heat. His shirt, somehow, was off; he had wriggled out of his pants. He didn't know this. All he knew was he had to get back to the hospital.

In the rearview mirror, the cabbie caught a glimpse of my friend, who was naked.

"GET OUT! GET OUT OF MY CAB, SIR! NO NAKED GUY IN MY CAB! OUT! *OUT!*"

My friend was back on his cell phone now, frantically

trying to get somebody at the hospital to come on the line. He didn't know he was naked; he barely realized he was being shoved naked into traffic by a hireling. The traffic, hostile, surged around him, drivers jeering him and honking their horns. Someone picked up his call.

"My mother!" he wept into the phone. "I'm in traffic—I'm *naked*—how's my mom?"

"I'm sorry, sweetheart. Your mother has passed."

My friend went blank.

"If it's any consolation, she was saying your name as she went."

Men's hands reached under his armpits then, one man per pit, and he was in the back of a squad car headed God knows where.

Next time I saw him, it was at a facility and he was dressed in one of those demi-length straitjackets. It was a while before things got normal again.

This is why, in the diner, I couldn't simply dismiss his feelings as the impossible plaint of an impossible personality.

My friend was silent and had been silent rather a long time. I studied his face and worried.

As I mentioned, he still looked murderous to me. I had all sorts of thoughts about that. I wondered, what happens to a murder deferred? He had no conventional feelings. He was not in woe. His eyes were prowling, there was a look of unfinished business about them. If you want to kill and the object of your bloodlust dies from natural causes, the homicidality doesn't just dry up, does it? It has to go somewhere. It has to find *someone else*, I thought.

Fortunately, breakfast arrived and we set on it. We talked fitfully and it was small talk. Ostensibly, we were there because his father had died and it didn't matter. We rode on that premise for the rest of the meal.

When we were done, we promised to speak to each other *hourly*, and he hugged me, which we both hated; it was as if we were imitating two other people.

That should have been the end of it, but for me there remained a sense of unease. I felt something was in the offing.

Every morning, I wake exhausted from the rigors of sleep—straining muscles, stiff joints, clogged sinuses—so when I awakened last week anxious, the feeling wasn't unfamiliar. When the anxiety converted to dread, I knew I had to act. It's a quirk of my personality that anytime I conceive the possibility of a new calamity, I imagine it's imminent; I imagine it's *happening*.

It was 3:23 a.m., according to my bedside digital, but who cared? He'd called me at similar hours.

"Who the fuck is this?"

"Thank God you're there."

"Jesus Christ!"

"Listen—"

"It's three-twenty-fucking-three in the morn—"

"*Listen* to me—"

"Are you out of your—"

"You have to promise me something."

"Do you know what *time* it—"

"Shut up! You have to *promise* me—"

"For crying out—"

"Listen!"

Silence.

"*What*?"

"Promise me that you won't kill Janette Sadik-Khan."

For a minute, I thought the line had gone dead.

"Are you fucking abusing *drugs*?"

"Please—just—please *say* it."

He let out a sigh; it was full of phlegm.

"I promise I will not kill Janette Sadik-Khan."

"*Thank* you."

"Eat me."

He hung up.

I wish my mind didn't have these lurid pockets. I was so certain I'd deduced his plan, and he'd never had any intention of the kind. His dismissiveness, his clear implication that I was cracked—these should mollify me, I know—they should put a period to my dread—yet somehow they don't.

I'm afraid I may have planted a seed.

On Liking
Racist Things

For fifteen years, from late youth to early middle age, I lived in an apartment complex called London Terrace. London Terrace is a vast Romanesque quadrangle that occupies the blocks from Twenty-Third to Twenty-Fourth Streets and from Ninth to Tenth Avenues in the Chelsea section of Manhattan. When I lived there, the apartments had multipaned windows that opened out from the middle and high ceilings and warped parquet floors, and the inward-facing apartments—I did not have one—looked out on a beautiful central courtyard that was very tranquil because nobody ever used it: all those prying eyes. Legend has it that the building opened in 1929 on the day of the Crash, and its original owner, ruined, jumped from a high window. I don't know if it was one of London Terrace's windows, although some of them are high up enough for that to have worked. The bulk of the apartments were rentals when I was there—only the corners were co-ops, with those people having special laundry room and swimming pool privileges that were taken away from the renters during my tenancy—but the renters gave the place a nice, middle-class, egalitarian air. Though children were in shorter supply than you'd imagine, there were plenty of dogs and they used the same elevators as the rest of us, which I found very pleasant; I like a good, quick visit with a dog.

My feeling for a neighborhood tends to be linear rather than rectangular, and when I lived in London Terrace, I traveled very far along Twenty-Third Street both east and west (there really isn't much west beyond Tenth Avenue) and knew almost nothing of Ninth Avenue, which in those days was still a little rough and undeveloped. Now I live around the corner from there and I walk along Ninth Avenue but hardly ever see Twenty-Third Street. Over the last decade, Ninth Avenue has turned into the more opportune street, with boutiques and restaurants and new construction both bad and less bad. When I was walking mostly on Twenty-Third Street, I had a singular relationship to the guy who lived in the apartment next to mine. We never went in the same direction. When I'd be walking west, he'd be walking east, when I'd be walking uptown, he'd be walking down, and, of course, vice versa. This happened three or four times a week for years and we never spoke of it—unwilling to break a spell, I guess—but as we passed, we'd give a sideways nod and a sly smile, to acknowledge the yoke of this peculiar, meaningless, and amusing destiny.

During the last months I lived on Twenty-Third Street, I met there a woman named Adele Persky Rincon Kramer. Actually, I think that's an abbreviation of her name. She'd been married several times, though never since I've known her, and along the way picked up and discarded a number of surnames. I can never remember them all, nor can I remember which husband was which and which name she was born with. It doesn't matter. She's a wonderful woman whatever she's called. We met because she'd seen a play of mine that was having a thwarted, heartbreaking production at the time, and she'd loved it, and had tickets to see it again, and she recognized me and *had to* tell me about it, so she just started talking. Liking something of mine that I'm not happy with is not a way to win me over—I'm prone to dress people down for it—but Adele is one of those rare, warm, starry people whom you can't help taking to on contact; or at least I can't.

She was in her early sixties at the time I met her and beautiful in that way you hardly see anymore: unretouched. Faces that age the way they're meant to have been so occluded in our imagination by the way famous women make their faces look—puffed and paved and slippery—that when you happen upon someone like Adele, not as naturally gorgeous as a movie star but vital and kind, you're dumbfounded by how attractive she is. Everything shows and you want to be near her.

Though she's not a chatterbox or a compulsive confider, by the end of that first meeting I knew about several of her husbands—she still liked them all—about her son who had just graduated from Harvard (after time out for a heroin addiction), and about a good swath of her history as social worker, amateur dancer, community activist, arts supporter, Grace Paley acquaintance, and general kibitzer.

So much depends on atmosphere. We met on a brilliantly sunny February afternoon and she wore a very pretty scarf—flowing, not the stunted, dismaying kind that's really a kerchief—and she was carrying two library books. It's the library books that got me. I don't know anyone else in the city who takes books out of the library, and public libraries have always paired in my mind with civic virtue. Adele struck me as the personification of this kind of virtue.

Also, it was a Sunday when we met, and though I am a free lance, Sunday is a freighted concept for me. There is a feature in the *New York Times* called "Sunday Routine." It's a half-page redacted Q & A with a public person who, typically, is on the oh-that-guy-he's-*who*-is-he-again? level of renown. I am *exactly* the type they come after, and I have this standing apprehension that someday, through the machinations of a PR person for some show I'm doing, I will be asked to answer the "Sunday Routine" questionnaire and have to agree or get a *reputation*. The only thing

I do on Sundays is read "Sunday Routine." It exhausts me for anything else because everyone they profile wakes at 6:45, makes coffee with a burr grinder, jogs around the Central Park reservoir, comes home, showers, goes for brunch, conducts the N.Y. Philharmonic, comes home again, throws a barbecue for fifty, and ends the day snuggling with the cat on a loveseat and watching *House of Cards*. If I'm asked, I'll have to aggregate memories of weekends going back about five years, then pretend they represent my typical Sunday, tra-la.

Or I could pretend to be Adele. *She* spends her Sundays doing all those sorts of things the WPA set in motion. She's at a free chamber concert or a museum or having a picnic in a lesser-known park or attending a lecture and being the one at the talk-back who's not offensive. When she walks along the street, her head is tilted up, she's heliotropic, and she smiles in an unforced way. Talking to you, she's all eagerness to get the best from you, and she makes being happy look easy the way Renée Fleming makes singing opera look easy. So much of talent is the absence of impediments and so much of life is devoted to cultivating impediments. If I could change my life condition in a single stroke, I would not choose to be envied or celebrated or even gaudily well-off. I would want to be filled with civic virtue like Adele and, like her, happy in a way that's not aware of itself.

Maybe I romanticize her; if so, it's just a little and because she was a benison during a time that was so disappointing. The show she liked that was so bad was not a bad play. It had had a production in Chicago the year before that was beautiful and had won acclaim so that people in New York were waiting for it, or, possibly, lying in wait for it, and the New York production turned out to be a feast for schadenfreude. Everything about it was off from the start. One of our actors, though a marvelous actor, was all wrong for the part and had to be let go late in rehearsals. Another actor, perfectly cast, suffered from a condition that caused her at an early preview to talk very, very slowly and mispronounce the other characters' names. She had to be replaced at intermission by an understudy who had never rehearsed and was a different body type and went onstage dressed in curtain material and bobby pins. There are gossip columnists whose beat is Broadway. They never have anything to write about so they wrote about us incessantly. On a Tuesday, the artistic director came into rehearsal, stood in front of the stage next to the play's director, and redirected the play. On Wednesday, the *New York Post* reported that the artistic director was standing next to the director and redirecting the play. That morning, the artistic director called to yell at me that the item had been planted by my agent. I told this to my agent, who yelled at me that he worked for me in a very pure way. I really hadn't done anything wrong, but everyone was yelling at me for some reason. So I yelled at the director. The play had elements of fantasy, and the plot turned on a crucial lighting effect, but the set was fussy and there was no wall space onto which the lighting effect could be projected, so no one had a clue what was going on. Audiences, who up to that point had been mostly indifferent, turned hostile. Because lumber is expensive while lighting is adjustable, instead of yelling at the set designer, everybody yelled at the lighting designer, who already resented me for yelling at the director and kept shooting me baleful looks. I got so depressed that on the day off, I bought an apartment.

I was coming from visiting that apartment—still months away from being habitable—when I met Adele and she told me how much she loved my sadly messed-up play. She could *hear* through the obscuring chaos of the production; she loved the *language*, she loved the *ideas*. This should have depressed me even more but, as I've said, it didn't.

We became friends after that day, though not steady friends—I had tea at her place once; she came to breakfast at mine. We spoke on the phone sometimes and e-mailed, and we always stopped to talk when we'd run into each other on the street.

I saw Adele on Ninth Avenue the other week and I have to say she didn't look like herself. The smile wasn't there and she seemed preoccupied—distracted, which she never is. She's always very much there with you. I was afraid for her. I thought possibly her son had had a relapse or she was sick. We went to the diner for coffee and I asked, gently, if something was wrong.

She laughed then, rather bitterly, I thought. Something *had* happened—a tiny thing, really not an event at all—and it made her question her sense of herself in a way she hadn't since . . . well, ever, really.

When I tell you what it was, please don't think less of her. Don't find her silly or overweening. I can assure you she's neither, and even though the situation she found herself in is something you or I would likely laugh off, it is not foolish that someone of Adele's age and with her history, and having lived through the larger history that she's lived through, would find it of concern.

Here it is. She was on the Internet several weeks ago and one of those mystifying, untraceable chains of links brought her to a YouTube video. It was Al Jolson singing "Mammy" in blackface. And she liked it.

Not ironically.

Jolson had been all the rage in the twenties and thirties but it is impossible to watch his minstrelsy now without thinking it unfathomably grotesque. It cannot be alibied into relevance. It's beyond excusing.

Adele found it mesmerizing. What's more, she found Jolson sexually compelling, ebonized skin, whitened lips and all. After playing the video, she played it again, then kept playing it for something like two hours. In bed that night, she thought of Jolson and his jazz hands and his knee drops and she found herself imagining his warm sweet breath on her neck and his jazz hands caressing her and holding her down. Over the next several days, she returned to the video compulsively, and when she took a day off, she missed Al Jolson with a feeling of nostalgia, of personal loss.

Adele had been married to a Colombian and dated a black man when black men were Negroes. She had linked arms and marched on Washington and once had a brief conversation with Eleanor Holmes Norton. Until this moment with Jolson, she had done these things unaffectedly. She was not self-conscious about them. She had never thought, "Here is my black friend; I am friend to a black person." The strands of her life were braided; it seemed obscene now to isolate them, to call upon a segment of this flowing, mingled history to give evidence that she was okay. Never before had she had to defend herself to herself. She was born a Jew, and one of her great joys had been the way Jews allied with blacks during the civil rights movement, and perhaps the greatest sadness came when that alliance ruptured.

And now: "Mammy."

I am too fallen a person to react to a story like this naturally. Obviously I wanted to laugh. Reverence for Adele held me in check. I tried to break it down for her. I told her I very much doubted that the racialist aspect of the piece was what was salient for her. Jolson was rated one of the greatest performers who ever lived. Magnetism can annul context. Yes, it's disturbing to love "Mammy" because "Mammy" is, well, so very ghastly, but she was probably seeing straight through the material to the performer. Had she tried viewing any other Jolson videos? Some showing him in his own white face, perhaps? Or was it possible— and maybe I was reaching here—that her father, whom she loved dearly and who died when she was seven, had sung "Mammy" to her when she was a small child? These Electra complexes were perfectly normal when the male parent has been snatched away too early. The most important thing was that she not let this revise her opinion of herself. She needed to apply the Whole Woman theory. Hers was a blameless, even a heroic life. Please smile, Adele.

Adele went to the ladies' room and I wiki'd Al Jolson on my phone. There, I found some surprising ammo, which I used when she returned.

And you know, Adele (I resumed), in his lifetime Jolson was a *hero* to black performers. They believed he paved the way for them, and they came in large numbers to pay their respects at his funeral. This just shows that the language of cultural transit is tricky and constantly mutating and one can be embraced and then shunned for the very same gesture. Isn't it possible, Adele, that this is at the root of the kinship you feel with Jolson and that your dreams are eroticizing it because that's what dreams do? I think that's it, Adele, I think we've found the key here.

Though she thanked me for my spiel, I'm not sure she was buying it. When I left her, she still wasn't quite Adele.

But her situation has made me think about the indefensible things I like. I yield to myself in a way that Adele's never had to because she is so naturally good and I'm not. And I've always resisted that popular trend of thought that holds efforts of questionable people to be necessarily contaminated. My sister-in-law for a time stopped reading Philip Roth after Claire Bloom published a book about what a rotten husband he'd been. How far can you take a thing like that? At London Terrace, I lived on the tenth floor and we had elevator men. What if it had turned out my elevator man was mean to his wife? Or a racist? I can climb a certain distance but I'm not good for ten floors. We live in a maculate world and the products we use have sometimes been worked on by loathsome people and are often themselves a mixed bag. Since talking to Adele, I've been making a list. It is a list of books and musicals and one TV show. Some of them are rancid with bigotry. Others— the musicals—are pure at heart and represent the best liberal thinking of their time, show-biz division. To quote, in augmented form, the great Oscar Hammerstein—who is not nicely treated further down—These are a few of my favorite racist things (and some I hate):

English Writers

I love Agatha Christie's novels, though I read somewhere that the versions I get have been expurgated of their anti-Semitic content.

Even so, an occasional bit of Jew-hating slips through.

I don't mind it. I don't think she meant it, really. I think for her, slagging Jews was like laying a cream tea or curtseying to the queen. It was simply part of her cultural dowry. You didn't question it.

G. K. Chesterton, on the other hand, was a real mouth-foamer when it came to the Jews. He was the author of many shapely causeries, as well as of the Father Brown mysteries, which I would enjoy very much were they not punctuated with vicious anti-Semitic jabs at the rate of roughly one every three paragraphs. These did not arise naturally. Chesterton had to go out of his narrative way to get in the comment about that grotesquely hooked nose or the mouth drooling lasciviously over a hillock of gold. He was rather psychotic on the issue. He might have ghost-written *The Protocols of the Elders of Zion*. He was an adept storyteller, but don't bother trying to get any pleasure out of him. He isn't worth it.

(Incidentally, you can go online and find a recent essay explaining why Chesterton was *not* an anti-Semite. It was written by an evangelical Christian and is itself a masterpiece of anti-Semitic rhetoric.)

Rodgers and Hammerstein Musicals

I have a friend named John who is half Japanese. He and his wife, Audrey, are very nice people, even square people. They attend church regularly and she is from the Midwest.

For years, I found it perplexing that John adamantly refused to tell me how the two of them met. There was some kind of shame attached to it.

It became such a mystery that for a while I considered looking at them in that way that is so fashionable in literature now—as People I Only Believe I Know But Are in Fact Unknowable. Just as a way to expand how I thought about what brought them together.

Maybe they'd met in rehab. Maybe in jail.

I'd just gotten to fisting bars when John blurted out:

"It was in a college production of *The King and I*!"

I had no reply to that.

"I would have *told* you if it had been a fisting bar," he said miserably.

You see, it galls him that he allowed himself to play the King of Siam. It grieves him that this production furnished the ground of his life's turning point. It makes him feel like a race traitor.

If you've forgotten, this is the story of *The King and I*:

A young and very hot king dies because a widowed British schoolmarm, whose main contribution to court life has been to instruct the palace chef that at state dinners he should serve bloody roast beef and a pie that tastes like urine instead of all that horrible *Thai* food, has said she doesn't like him anymore.

They're so *sensitive*, those Asian despots.

But for all that, *The King and I* has very pretty music and ample pageantry, and a recent superlative production brought out complexities of feeling that may or may not have been latent in the script.

I don't think the same is possible for *South Pacific*. Even in the finest production imaginable, there's almost nothing I like about *South Pacific*. Every song in it is famous, but most of them are dirges. You could probably score six or seven funerals out of that show without repeating.

There are a plot and subplot to *South Pacific* and both of them are deplorable.

Here is the plot:

Aging French planter Emile de Becque has fallen in love

with a young nurse from Arkansas named Nellie Forbush. She is an idiot. When the magnificent singing actress Kelli O'Hara played her, her every line reading gave the impression that she was striving to say something better. It was as if she couldn't believe how terrible her dialogue was.

All the same, when the American military asks de Becque to join them on a dangerous mission that could turn the tide of the war (he has some sort of dubious expertise they don't), he refuses, too besotted with the little twit to risk his life in the Allied cause.

Nellie loves him right back, even after he confides that when he was young, he killed a man. He explains this in the sort of simple, primer-like sentences she can understand.

"I killed a man. He was a bad man."

All very *Dick, Jane, and Sally Off Their Neighbor.*

But there's trouble ahead. Because, though human snuffing is acceptable to her, Nellie cannot bear it when she learns that Emile has procreated with a Polynesian woman, physically recoiling at the thought of being impaled upon the dick that touched the yellow girl's pudenda.

This leaves Emile devastated. Right away, he alerts the Marines that he's changed his mind and is willing to risk his life on the patriotic mission. For without the young Arkansan, what has he to live for (his two small, motherless children evidently not being of concern)?

Thus he meets up with the subplot, in the person of

Lieutenant Joe Cable, a gleaming slab of Princeton-trained sirloin who has been doing time as our Juvenile Lead.

Joe, who is somewhat priggish and uptight, not to mention engaged to a Philadelphia girl, has already discovered a Great Impossible Love of his own.

While taking a little R and R on the island of Bali Ha'i, he has been intercepted by the Tonka woman Bloody Mary, who is always chewing betel nut though she don't use Pepsodent. Like everybody else in this musical, she swales all over the lieutenant's to-die-for torso (Joshua Logan directed the original production) and immediately introduces him to a lovely young Polynesian girl, Liat, who appears to be domiciled in a cave. She is also Bloody Mary's jail-bait daughter. Liat and Cable take one look at each other, exchange a darling little bit of sign language, and upon Bloody Mary's retreat, get down to having wild, anonymous sex.

After the fucking, Joe looks at Liat's face for the first time and says, "Why, you're just a kid!" then sings "Younger Than Springtime."

This was Penn State pedophile Jerry Sandusky's big mistake. He should have sung "Younger Than Springtime" at those little boys when he was done with them. Everything might have gone so differently if he had.

Anyway, long story short: Joe and his family are too racist for him to dump his frigid Philadelphia fiancée in favor of the underage Polynesian chick; he and de Becque go on the mission together; he's killed, de Beque survives.

Meanwhile, Nellie, in worrying about Emile, has learned her life's great lesson—it is possible to love a very wealthy French planter even if he has been in congress with a gook—they return to each other, and we're all better people for it.

When *South Pacific* was written, the great liberal watchword was "tolerance."

That's such a sweet thing to say to somebody:

I *tolerate* your negritude.

I *tolerate* your Tonkinesiness.

A Sitcom

On television, the most racist show in history was the inexplicably esteemed *The Golden Girls*.

Cunningly, the ethnicity being disparaged was Minnesotan, so it was possible to have all the fun of racism with none of the blowback.

Two Classics

I forgive F. Scott Fitzgerald for Meyer Wolfsheim because *The Great Gatsby* is a fantastic novel and Wolfsheim, once you get past the anti-Semitism from which he sprang, is a marvelous character.

I *don't* forgive Ernest Hemingway for Robert Cohn because the last time I read it, *The Sun Also Rises* struck me as a ridiculous book.

[**OBLIGATORY**]

My Best Recipe

When they put out a new edition of *Mein Kampf,* it will include a few recipes—Hitler's Sunday Spaetzel and things like that. All books need recipes now, and who am I to buck a trend?

This is the best recipe I ever invented. I think it's a very modern recipe because, though on the face of it it's easy and abandoned, when you get down to making it, it's persnickety and creates a lot of tension.

It has only two ingredients. "Two ingredients!" I can hear Ina Garten exclaim in her beloved Connecticut simper. "How easy is that?"

Wait.

The two ingredients are parsley and grapefruit juice.

However, while the grapefruit juice may come from a container, it must come from a certain *kind* of container. The word "Tropicana" must not appear on it. The words "Fresh-Squeezed" and "Organic" must.

Even then, you'll want to yank some juice from an actual ruby red or pink grapefruit, for decency's sake.

And the parsley, of course, is the flat leaf—or Italian—kind. I don't even know why they still bother growing the curly stuff; it must have something to do with crop rotation.

You take the flat-leaf parsley and the grapefruit juice and whoosh them in a blender. Then you strain the purée through a fine-mesh sieve.

Candidly, though? A chinois would work way better than the sieve. It'll only cost you a couple hundred bucks.

When it's absolutely free of fiber, you refrigerate the strained product until it's bristling-cold. Then you pour it over vanilla ice cream, and eat.

It will be a very emotional experience for you. It will make you think of the first scent of spring on the just-warming winter air on a day when you were young, and it will make you think of fields of hollyhocks and losing your innocence, and you will brush away a tear at the thoughts but be so grateful for that tear, deeply, deeply grateful.

Only here's the thing.

You can't whoosh the stuff the day before or even earlier in the day, really. You have to wait until, at the earliest, right before you sit down to dinner. This isn't so onerous except you'll be very sad for the whole meal thinking of all the parsley guck sticking to the blender blades and what a nightmare cleaning up is going to be.

Also, the grapefruit is acidic, which will turn the ice cream into soup. This is okay as you're finishing but not what you want when you start, so if you're serving it to guests you need to pass it around in a sauce boat and give them meticulous instructions as to how to proceed.

Actually, what you *should* do is scoop the ice cream into bowls *before* dinner and place the bowls in the freezer to get them extremely cold. You may have to buy one of those country house–scaled side-by-side refrigerator-freezers for this.

Another thing: you'll need to *insist* that each guest starts in on his or her dessert the second it's been assembled; there's to be no waiting for the whole table to be served.

And if some of your guests refuse because they have too bone-deep a sense of etiquette, you'll have to watch as they slurp what has become a soup too early, then pretend that they're enjoying it in the complex, rhapsodic way you meant for them to enjoy it.

The performance will be overwrought or halfhearted and it will enrage you, because their obstinacy is registering as your failure.

And that is—in a word—unfair.

Maeve and Fredda

I have known two women who went mad. One was a friend I met when I was at grad school, the other a writer I knew— and know—only through her work. What, at their best, they shared, aside from my affection for them, was a profound moral vision, an inerrant feel for the essence of things, far beyond what others could see or be made to see. So strong was this gift in both of them, and so total their collapse, that it's hard not to believe that the gift and the collapse were fatally linked, inexorable, as though the weight of this Cassandra power became too heavy to bear.

This, obviously, is artsy bull. No one goes mad from excessive clarity. There are clinical roots to it, probably chemical ones. I'm chasing after a thesis that will join them because I want to write about them together—because it seems to me, obscurely, that they *belong* together, in their sanity as well as in their madness.

"Madness," too, smacks of melodrama, summoning lurid nineteenth-century images of storms and moors and women with wild tresses. "Mental illness," equally lacking in content, is better. There's a level, scientific sound about it, a detachment.

So then: these two women suffered mental illness, brought on by psychosocial chemical disruptions or eruptions.

This part is not my subject.

Fredda I first knew during the early eighties in New Haven. She was Jim's wife. This was part of the problem and only in part a problem. They had met at Emerson College, where they were theater majors, Fredda pursuing a concentration in directing, Jim in playwrighting. At Yale, Jim was the unrivaled star of the department. He'd read everything and his plays showed it. They were farcical, lyrical, bawdy, sentimental. He wrote a dramatic vaudeville about Guiteau, the assassin of Garfield, as well as a musical cabaret that featured a long-lost rock journalist named Shirley Esther Fliegelman. (I named her; in the program I was credited as "Yiddish Dramaturg.") He was tall, with a beer gut no longer attributable to beer, a splay-footed walk different from but as bizarre as my own. People often took him for an albino—he was excluded from albinism by about a gram of melanin. He smoked incessantly. Bashful, he hid behind tinted glasses, looking to the side of you or at the floor. Women found him attractive.

Fredda was five years younger than Jim, but Jim, delayed by alcoholism, ended up in her class.

I first became aware of Maeve Brennan when a friend directed me to her stories about a town called Herbert's Retreat, a barely fictionalized version of Snedens Landing, where she had lived during her brief marriage to fellow *New Yorker* writer St. Clair McKelway, who was older than Maeve, and notorious at the magazine for his drinking and sexual incontinence.

That must have been a very unhappy marriage and Maeve must have hated every last thing about Snedens Landing. The Herbert's Retreat stories are mean. Vicious, really. Maeve had an elephantine memory for episodes of pettiness that she'd witnessed or borne the brunt of during her childhood. A vein of tender indignation runs through most of her work. There is no tenderness in the Herbert's Retreat stories, just lynx-eyed sketches of rich people who hide their peasant origins and broke people covering up their poverty. The propertied are pretentious and cruel, their Irish maids gossipy and bitter. Singularly lacking in these stories is the quality of admiration—even of the mordant kind we extend to clever scoundrels. There are scoundrels galore in Herbert's Retreat but they are not clever.

They are bad, incompetent scoundrels. Not only did Maeve find nothing to admire in them, she, uncharacteristically, found nothing to forgive. The Herbert's Retreat stories are deft, and scabrous and hilarious, and the worst things she ever wrote. She invented transparent characters, then saw through them. This, I would later discover, was not her way.

Though nasty, the Herbert's Retreat stories were tantalizing enough to make me investigate this Maeve Brennan further. I learned that she had been a highly regarded short-story writer, at least one of whose stories, "The Springs of Affection," was counted among the greatest of the century. There was also a book of essays called *The Long-Winded Lady*.

Fredda loved doing antic, disruptive things on the street. She was great at pratfalls, if there were people there to see. I've always tried to disappear in public and sometimes would walk several strides ahead of her, in fear that she'd be struck by inspiration.

"Don't you walk away from me!" she'd cry, all lofty outrage. "This is *your baby*!"

The Long-Winded Lady is a collection of pieces written for the *New Yorker*'s "Talk of the Town" section, the section at the front of the magazine devoted to casual essays. They were written over two decades, starting in the mid-fifties—a few more came later—and the book belongs to a category I may have made up: The Inadvertent Masterpiece. These are books that collect bits and pieces of writing composed over years, often for money, and not aimed at a book, but unified by the strength of the writer's voice. In Maeve's case, that voice is one of the supplest, smartest, most tender I know. It's difficult to describe these essays. They sound trivial. They're not.

The long-winded lady (the eponym was assigned her by the section's editor) tells us what she saw while she was walking in the street or eating in a restaurant. She considers inexpensive neighborhood restaurants "the home fires" of New York City. She is obviously something of a displaced person, at least to a degree by election. She calls herself a "traveler-in-residence," living in hotels most of the time, at first in Greenwich Village, later in the seedier lodgings of late-sixties and early-seventies Times Square—near her office at the *New Yorker*; even so . . .

She has lived in and walked through these neighborhoods long enough to remember and lament what in them has gone missing. She feels she is always one step ahead of the wrecking ball and that the places she has loved are being stalked by "the ogre called office space."

If you read *The Long-Winded Lady* all the way through (as opposed to dipping into it), you recognize that it is an informal natural history of the city—of, at least, a few loved neighborhoods of the city. You also realize that its author, zigzagging among sublets and hotel quarters, carries with her an acute sense of home. It's somewhere else.

We are not given too many details about the personal lives of "Talk of the Town" authors. This worked to the advantage of the long-windeds, reinforcing their panoptical quality. Maeve witnesses—loving, stern, judicious, she *bears* witness, and she triangulates. Fundamentally unconnected events gain meaning in relation to one another because she sees them unfold at the same time, or because an incident recalls an earlier incident. She likes to draw morals from these associations, often playfully elusive ones. I've always thought of her as a kind of urban displacement of Emerson's transparent eyeball. She is a conduit—the operations of the city are revealed through her.

Fredda did herself up like a bohemian—the eighties kind of bohemian; she could have been an extra in *Desperately Seeking Susan*—but she was a bohemian by conscription. Once I heard her say to Jim, in passing, "We need to have sex every night this month so I can get pregnant." She dreamed of babies and little houses in the suburbs. About her degree of professional ambition I was never sure.

When Jim's mood darkened, turned illegible, she pined. "Why can't everything just be *easy*?"

During the first Christmas season of her crisis, when she was in New York, moving among friends' apartments, a friend of mine and I took her to see *It's a Wonderful Life*. Bedford Falls and all those loving neighbors. She couldn't stop crying.

"Why can't life really *be* like that?"

From Angela Bourke, Maeve's biographer, we learn that Maeve's father was a distinguished Irish politician and, for a time, something of a casualty of Irish history. For his role in the Easter Uprising of 1916, he was sentenced to death; he was in prison when Maeve was born. The sentence was commuted and, eventually, he became an envoy to Washington. The family moved there in 1934, when Maeve was seventeen.

Maeve abominated the heat. She thought of smothering in it, and a hot day brought "powerful gusts of memory" of other hot days.

She loved when the heat would remit and the weather become "a miracle in itself."

There used to be an Italian restaurant on Twenty-Third Street between Ninth and Tenth. A red-sauce place where the waiter had brilliantined hair, they filleted the fish tableside, and the walls were covered in decorative tile, it opened forty years too late and never caught on. I adored it.

One day in summer, a day when the heat had remitted, I met a friend there for lunch. The front door was open. (Maeve had lunched on a day like this at a restaurant like this; they had left the door open there, too, and she approved the choice.) There was only one other customer in the restaurant, a friendly-looking woman, thin and middle-aged, who wore a sundress and a straw hat and read a book as she ate. That section of Twenty-Third Street is almost entirely residential, and on a half-warm, half-cool summer afternoon, you can convince yourself you're not in the city at all, at least not in the present-day city. The street has a private tempo, an almost Southern sashay.

It *was* the city, but the city in, say, 1953. I looked at the woman lunching alone and thought of Maeve.

While Jim was being the most dazzling member of our playwrighting class, Fredda worked as a receptionist down the road, at a famous regional theater. The theater was in a building connected to an abattoir that had a window in front through which you could see gutted cows hanging from hooks.

Fredda did get to direct once, at the Yale Cabaret. It was a production of a beautiful student play called *Terminal Bar* that had originally been put up as a first-year project. She did a superb job. She was really very talented.

My father has never been a self-starter, so after my mother died, my brother, my sister-in-law, and I tried to get him interested in something. About a decade ago, I formed a book club with him and a couple of kind friends. That lasted a few sessions. Four years ago, I restarted it. This time he and I were the only members. The first book I assigned us was *The Long-Winded Lady*. His reaction was not unrepresentative of the responses this book gets.

He liked it but suspected he shouldn't.

After all, this was not Important Literature. No one died in a foxhole or painted the ceiling of the Sistine Chapel.

"How much of your life," I asked him, "has been devoted to significant events?"

"Maybe five percent," he said.

I told him I thought he was overestimating and asked if he believed that the bulk of his—and everyone's—life should be off-limits to literature.

He shrugged and hemmed and conveyed that he thought probably it should.

One of the pieces in *The Long-Winded Lady* is about

breaking the heel of a new shoe. In another, she orders broccoli and forgets which end you're supposed to eat (it's both, but never mind). Sometimes, she is on the way to an event; she is never *at* an event. Maeve was a chronicler of the non-moment, a poet of the interim.

In our second year in New Haven, Patti and I lived on the other side of the wall from Jim and Fredda. They had lived far from campus before that, and the move was liberating for Fredda. She became a doyenne. Their apartment was the place where everyone gathered.

Jim and Fredda smoked constantly. In the early eighties, this was still a glamorous activity. People who didn't smoke, like me, thought nothing of hanging out in rooms that were stale and cloudy with cigarette fume.

Friends from Emerson were always visiting. One day, I was shaving and singing in the bathroom. From the other side of the medicine chest, a thrilling soprano joined in. We finished our duet and a little while later, I met her. This was Beth, who was tall and willowy and red-haired with a beautiful Modigliani face. Funny, whip-smart. Good-crazy.

The people you met at drama school could be a little high-strung. Fredda tended to them—to us. She adjudicated our disputes. She had common sense. She was a tad heavy, and at home tended to dress like Stritch, long white oxford shirts over black tights. She had great, skinny legs.

She was good-crazy, too, at times, but she was our rock.

Maeve was tiny and beautiful with a piquant Irish face, locket-ready, and an updo. As her tether loosened, the updo rose. There is a photograph from the seventies when she was living by the water. Her hair had passed beehive and attained silo.

In the city, in the early days, she had been a fashion writer, her grooming always exquisite.

On Joan Didion's mother's refrigerator, there was a sampler with the embroidered homily "God Is Love."

Didion shuddered whenever she saw it because it seemed to her that when her mother was brutally murdered, the reporter writing about the case would seize on this sampler as the perfect ironic detail with which to end his account of the crime.

A group of us had stayed in New Haven to work at the Summer Cabaret. After the second show on July Fourth, we were walking on campus. We sang "The Star-Spangled Banner." This was neither earnest nor satirical—we didn't know what it was. As we finished, two suspicious-looking young men, townies and ruffians, we thought, approached us. Fredda narrated:

"Here the mass murderers are coming to kill us, and we've just sung 'The Star-Spangled Banner'—that will be the ironic detail."

They bummed a light off Jim and moved on. The show that opened that night had been written by Jim—a comic take on *Dracula*.

Later, in Jim and Fredda's apartment, there were bats, flying near the ceiling—in their apartment: bats!

Fredda went crazy because Jim cheated on her. We never quite blamed him for this, though we blamed his consort, cattily, without mercy.

It happened the year after graduation. Jim and Fredda had stayed on in New Haven for a reason I no longer remember. The affair was with an actress two classes behind ours. During the post-graduation year, the actress had become friendly with Fredda as well. After the affair was revealed, Fredda promoted her to her "best" friend. This was a dramaturgical decision; it raised the stakes.

All right, then. Fredda went crazy because Jim cheated on her, but—really?

Women who have been cheated on become "wrathful." They grow "embittered." They find they "can no longer trust." They enter a "period of depression."

Crazy, though?

Obviously, there were other factors in play. A complicated childhood, probably a traumatic one. Parents divorced, father a Sabra. Something happened in Israel. Dimly, I recall explicit references made in my presence as to what. I chose not to hear them. They were too dire, hard to believe. Criminal.

Also, there was her mother. I met her mother a few times, a nice woman from suburban Boston, mildly kooky, very personable. When Fredda was a teenager, her mother snapped. Went loony. Emergency help was called. Somehow the men in the white coats got it into their heads that *Fredda* was the crazy one. Her frantic explanations as they endeavored to cart her off (I always picture butterfly nets) only proved their point. A funny, Kafkaesque episode.

So there was that.

That Fredda went into the kind of tailspin she did made no sense, but at least there was an inciting event.

Maeve, not so much.

As things became tense, but before Fredda knew why, I visited them in New Haven, summoned by Fredda. Jim, who loved me, made it clear that he was not happy to have me. Fredda and I went to the play at the Rep, an Ibsen with a domestic setting. At the rear of the stage, hanging high, looming over everything, was an enormous skeletal sculpture of a horse.

I worked with this.

It's a Pegasus image, I told myself. The play is about overvaulting ambition, its damage. The protagonist embodies hubris, he is unaware of the destruction he is wreaking all about him. It's a Pegasus-*cum*-Icarus image. He is flying too close to the sun, incinerating all he loves . . .

Midway through the first act, Fredda leaned over to me and whispered, "Why is there a horse in their living room?"

Our first year in Manhattan, Patti and I lived in a tall, vaguely fancy building that called itself a mews—New York's most vertical mews—and was full of hookers. My bed was in the bedroom, hers in the living room. She made her New York debut in a so-so revival of a deservedly forgotten comedy; the response was indifferent. Somehow this led to a blowup between us. I wandered around the city all the next day so as not to deal with her. When she came home from the performance that night, we apologized to each other, then the phone rang.

Jim and Fredda. They were at Grand Central Station. Could they come to us?

It all spilled out. (Patti had guessed it months ago; I hadn't believed her.) They'd left New Haven on a frenzied impulse, New Haven was where the evil was. They slept in Patti's bed, Patti slept in my bed, I slept on the couch.

At six the next morning I was nudged awake. Fredda was looking down at me.

"Do you want to go for a walk?"

Yes, yes, I did. I just needed a minute to dress.

Up and down Broadway Fredda howled out jungle

noises. Passersby blamed me. Later, laughing, she told me that wouldn't be happening again, she'd had a *huge* epiphany. This sequence would be repeated I don't know how many times, over countless weeks.

Once, as I walked on Broadway with Jim, he allowed that he and Fredda were at least "Platonic fifths."

Maeve wrote less frequently. She became harder to find. She made money but was wildly generous and always lacked money. Her impeccable grooming first became outdated, then became less impeccable. People whispered that she was behaving erratically. At one point, in the night, an office at the *New Yorker* was vandalized. It was repaired the next morning without comment.

One day, when she was staying with other people, during the early part of her breakdown, Fredda stopped by our apartment to break down some more. She wailed and lamented. In the middle of this, Patti and I began to spat. The cause was trivial—we were young and broke and tense. Fredda, who had suspended her lament, started to laugh, and interrupted us. "You *guys*," she said, "you're both being idiots." With cold logic, she explained why what we were saying to each other was inane. We conceded the point and she went back to wailing.

The last pieces in *The Long-Winded Lady* are heartbreaking. Maeve is so helplessly loving, but to whose benefit? She describes the past in crystal detail—did she know where the present was? A few pieces from a decade earlier may already show signs of unraveling. They are filled with darting, cryptic images. In one, she's staying in her friend Howard's apartment. There's a cocktail party across the hall and a rainstorm. The writing is private and unbelievably gorgeous—but is it the privacy of someone who is already retreating from the actual world? Is this the Maeve who would meet with a friend for lunch and seem her irresistible self, then start talking about the ones who were after her—"You *know* who I mean"?

Then again, it might just be a question of style. Maeve's talent was essentially poetic, and who can say when a poet's gone crazy?

Thinned by grief, Fredda's body became the ideal of an earlier decade. She was an Italian movie star from the fifties—bosomy, with hips—va-va-va-voom. Women no longer aspired to this figure; men still preferred it. Churning with rage, with obsession, with disbelief, she nevertheless used the power her new body afforded her. She dressed up. I remember one dress in particular: heather green in some sort of stretchy, clingy material. She wore it with a fat leather belt and a necklace chunky with wood and glass ornaments. We sat in the window of a diner on Broadway in the Fifties and she nipple-smoked cigarette after cigarette. As I remember them, they were all butts, as though she'd foraged her cigarettes from public ashtrays. She had plans for dating. She wasn't going to let anyone near her unless he bought her presents, *expensive* presents, *lots* of them. She gazed out at Broadway. Her reflection smeared in the window in the blue afternoon light.

Her face was stricken, lovely, her bobbed hair bleached a streaky white, albino-white with dun-colored roots. She was ragged, sizzling, beaten, forlorn. The scene was period, perfect. She looked like an untaken photograph. There should have been a saxophone.

When Fredda was staying with Timo and Paul, they could hear her all night, smoking and pacing and muttering.

Muttering in Hebrew.

The New York exile went on and on. The idea was, Fredda's fate hinged on Jim's decision: Would he stay married to her?

He didn't know, he wasn't sure.

She managed to get a job as a room-service waitress at the Marriott Marquis, a white deco fart of a hotel in Times Square. She came to us after her shift. Her server's coat was disgustingly stained with hours-old food spillage. She had blubbered her way through the evening. By the time the guests were done consoling her, their burgers had gone cold.

Jim didn't know, he wasn't sure.

His Hamletting around wore on everyone's nerves.

One day, Patti swept the floor with short, vindictive strokes.

Jim—she told the air—I love ya, baby, but you've gotta shit or get off the pot! (*Sweep.*) Shit or get off the pot!

I don't care if he stays with her! (*Sweep.*)

I don't care if he leaves her! (*Sweep.*)

I don't care if he KILLS her! (*Sweep.*)

But he's gotta shit or get off the pot! (*Sweep.*) Shit or get off the pot!

Solitary, Maeve continued her walks through the city. Once, in front of the New York Public Library, she saw a patch of light on the sidewalk that had been transported, lock, stock, and barrel, from her childhood home in Ireland.

In Fredda's salon in New Haven, the topic of suicide. Funny, louche-glamorous Cathy, a costume designer who would go on to win about a thousand Tony awards, offered that she couldn't imagine killing herself because there'd always be movies she'd want to see.

"But you probably wouldn't want to see any of the movies," suggested Fredda.

Fredda's last call came from the institution where she was bivouacked, in Massachusetts, I think. By then, she was pure grief; finished. It was not any longer dramatic. She didn't make those deep, barreling noises or the high, keening ones. She didn't hoot out tears. The pain now was distracted; at times, she was flippant about it. She spoke of an affair she was having (maybe) with some preppy kid she thought was "out of his mind." She asked if I knew how she could get her hands on barbiturates. You needed a lot of them to kill yourself and they were really hard to get ahold of. Common wisdom back then maintained that if they *spoke* about it, they didn't *do* it, so this was reassuring, if anything. We continued to banter about pills for a while, then I got a call-waiting. With some strategy, I couldn't find a writing utensil to take down her number. "Please, Fredda," I implored her, "call me later, will you? *Will* you?"

Yeah, yeah, she said. Distracted.

Maeve tried moving back to Ireland, where she stayed with family. She was welcomed, treated well, but sealed herself off from them, holed up in her room, typing. She'd forget the kettle on the stovetop, the water would boil away. She thought she was married to a man, possibly James Joyce, and was the mother of many children, "boys and girls." She was a loner among her own people. She came back to New York.

I had had a not-so-difficult evening with someone with whom I'd been having many difficult evenings and came home to this on the phone machine: "Rich, it's Beth—call me!" I checked the clock—it was 11:26, too late to call.

Beth answered on the first ring.

"Oh God, Rich, Fredda killed herself!"

Jim had returned to his apartment and this was on his machine: "Jim, this is your dad. Come home immediately. Your wife has killed herself." All he could think was: *I have to erase this message.*

Fredda's mother was called in to identify the body.

A corpse, left a bit too long to fester, will change appearance.

"This isn't my daughter!" she cried. "This is a black woman!"

The offices of the *New Yorker* are a courtly place where, when a madwoman passes through, gentlemen acknowledge her with a polite nod, provided she's a madwoman on the payroll.

Younger female employees were often shaken to see a homeless woman sleeping in the ladies' room. They were counseled to show tolerance. But she was so disheveled, so badly made-up.

You know a woman's crazy when the lipstick *circles* the lips.

Fredda had written a general suicide note that was read at the funeral. Later, at the shiva, twenty-three of us were taken discreetly aside and given personalized suicide notes. Mine said: "Always remember the green beans."

On desultory afternoons in New Haven, Fredda and I sometimes sat in my living room, eating raw green beans from a colander. Fredda brought to the activity a campy, regal air. "More green beans, Rich!" she'd command as rations ran low, and I would fetch them from the kitchen. For some reason, we always remembered these occasions as a highlight of our time together at Yale.

Even so, I have to admit I was disappointed in my suicide note. It was a bit too yearbook-y for my taste. I wondered if Fredda had written it late in the composition process, when inspiration was fading, and if that meant I had been a low priority for her, twenty-first or twenty-second of the twenty-three. Possibly, I had just barely made the cut.

When Fredda killed herself, Patti was filming two movies, and on the day of the funeral she was set to shoot in San Francisco. She beseeched the producer to let her out.

He was sympathetic but this was the more expensive of the films, a Clint Eastwood, and there was no slack in the schedule. Because we lived together, I was given custody of her suicide note.

I was a conscientious guardian of that note. I kept it always in a pants pocket. At the end of the day, I would transfer it to the pants I was going to wear the next day. When Patti returned from making her movies, I asked if she wanted to see her suicide note. She said she needed to work her way up to it. I traveled back and forth a few times from Seattle, where I had a play in its first production. After the opening, I returned to New York and went with my friend Lisa to see a Gorky play at NYU. Before it started, I reached into my pocket to get Tic Tacs, and went suddenly cold. We didn't have cell phones then. I found a pay phone on Eighth Street.

"Patti—Jesus!—I've lost your suicide note!"

Maeve was somehow brought into the care of social agencies. She lived in a hospital or a home, an institution of some kind. There is a piece in the expanded edition of *Long-Winded* in which she writes that it is ninety-four degrees out, a dreadful day in New York City, but that the air-conditioning is producing ocean breezes. The description of the bed has caused some readers to believe the piece was written from a hospital room.

After Fredda died, there was much concern about Jim's sobriety. He did great. Rebuilt his life. Nice girlfriends. A brief remarriage. He moved to L.A., became a successful screenwriter, made money, rented an expensive architect house. Ten years in, he wrote his first play since drama school. You could tell it had started as a screenplay, something of a genre piece, a Boston crime suspencer. There was the character of the crazy, abandoned wife. She was a flashing, inflamed, intrusive character—a traffic light in search of an intersection. Jim needed her in the play more than the play did.

In the middle of working on the play, Jim had to fly somewhere, always a trying thing for him. It occurred to him he could handle a single drink. He could not. Beth and Sheryl—I'd first met Sheryl in the van taking us from the funeral to the shiva—saw him through the mawkish, physically gross crack-up.

While he was drinking, he stopped meeting deadlines, could no longer be hired. He went broke. He moved to Saugerties, New York, did some landscaping work, became involved with a very nice woman he'd met in AA.

Tessie called me. Things didn't look good. Jim had been stricken with cancer of all the organs he hadn't abused. On the way to the hospital to die, he freaked out. The palliative drugs were making him high. He was concerned for his sobriety.

When I think of what I have to say about Fredda, it doesn't seem sufficient. She dressed this way, she said those clever things, this is what happened to her. She might be some composite girl from the eighties, a little unstable, none too vivid. There might have been a dozen Freddas, a thousand. But this is what I remember of her, this is *how* I remember her. She was twenty-eight years old when she killed herself. Did she have time to become specific?

Even when I'm on the streets—Midtown, Broadway— where she had her breakdown next to me, they don't make me think about her. They're the same streets Maeve wrote about. I think, instead, of what Maeve wrote. I can't correct that. All I can say is, of the thousand Freddas, this one was ours.

I don't have to worry about diminishing Maeve, because where Fredda left nothing behind, Maeve left her books. She's safe from me.

The impressionist Rich Little once said that when he imitated Robert Goulet he could reach notes that were not in his own voice. In a college acting class, we were assigned the task of answering questions as someone else. I chose my best friend at the time, a guy who was much quicker and much funnier than I was, and I became much quicker and funnier than myself. Now, when I am in certain neighborhoods, or when the heat is unbearable in a period way, or when strangers on the street who are unaware of each other simultaneously perform intricate and mysterious tasks, I become Maeve. I make the sentences I believe she would make and I am shrewder than myself and kinder and more observant and more eloquent, and the present moment, which might otherwise overwhelm me, fills with radiance.

It's transporting.

In Order of Disappearance

I work chiefly as a playwright—some years, I even make my living as a playwright—and God knows casting is hard enough already, so it's not in my best interest to point out that several women who acted in my plays, and became my friends, died young, or, if not young, early. I'm doing it anyway because I want to say a word about each of them, and I'm willing to risk the ensuing boycott.

Miranda

I can remember doing only one intelligent thing in my twenties and it still baffles me that, in that era of otherwise unblemished stupidity, I was capable of it. It happened the summer after I graduated drama school. In the last months of school, I'd had a one-act play in New York that had created a stir—this was possible in those days.

Coincidentally, the American film industry was then enjoying the most slap-happy, fiscally irresponsible moment in its medium-long history. One film was made for every hundred put into development. This created a voracious hunger for writers, and I was summoned to four or five meetings a week in those Midtown towers where the studios' New York offices were located then. Every office had the identical breathtaking view; it was of one another's towers. That view started to look banal to me very quickly. The meetings were with duos of Bright Young Development People who, after offering coffee or "a water" and exchanging a little byplay about the provenance of their suits, would ask me what sort of screenplay I wanted to write. I had very little interest in writing any sort of screenplay, though I had an enormous interest in getting *paid* for writing screenplays, and I always fumbled this question. No matter. The BYDP had ideas of their own.

Why not try a fish-out-of-water story?

A few years before, *Splash*, a story about an actual fish out of real salt water, had come from nowhere to earn mountains of money, and it had been the working paradigm ever since. You could not, however, simply rip off *Splash* and call it a day. You had to disguise what you were doing, in a transparent way, and to this end, the BYDP set themselves up as a kind of matchmaking service, brokering unions between gigantic hits of recent vintage—this supplied the fig leaf of originality that kept Legal at bay. It wasn't exactly burdensome. When it came time to pitch to the important people, all you had to do was say, "It's *Trading Places* meets *Gandhi*," and everyone would be deliriously happy and give you money.

Several weeks into this process, I had my moment of intelligence. It was a weekday afternoon in Brooklyn Heights, where Patti and I had found a sublet to see us through August, by which point, presumably, we'd have signed a lease on the apartment in Manhattan where we'd start our real lives. I was detained at a Don't Walk sign after returning from a morning meeting at Fox or Columbia or Tri-Star, probably the third or fourth meeting of identical character I'd had that week. Out of nowhere, I said to myself, "Years from now, you're going to want to be nostalgic about this time. Just remember: you're not having much fun."

I've always been grateful for this bit of prescience. However grisly the present may get, I'm never tempted to revel in the past because the past sent me explicit instructions not to.

Disenchantment comes quickly to the foolish and the lazy—the instant we realize that our heart's desire doesn't come by way of abracadabra, but stepwise, with many of the steps leading in the wrong direction. After a few weeks, I was tired of the subway, of being broke, of sweating in the heat. I resented having to write a comedy about rebels from a fictitious Spanish-speaking country staging a military coup in Palm Beach. It didn't seem at all my kind of thing.

But nobody was buying the story I'd come up with on my own. That was a rollicking farce about the pirate invasion of a ship full of opera singers. I called it *Trouble on the High Cs*. It would have been good.

All in all, it was a dreary time and an annulment of the dream of the city I'd been steadily cultivating for twenty years, from early childhood, and that had gotten a kind of encouragement just a few weeks before, the afternoon I'd spent with Miranda.

She had been one of the stars of that one-act play. She was young, younger than I was—by how many years has been called into question—pretty by real-world standards, if those standards still obtained even then, certainly attractive by any sane estimation. She was an eighties type, though we didn't know that then, buoyant, spiky, moderately streetwise. Apt to dress in mixed denims and a scrunchie.

I barely remember what we did that afternoon. I know we walked around a bit, had lunch at one of those eighties Upper West Side restaurants where the tables were covered in white butcher paper and cups of crayons were provided so that full-fledged adults could color as they ate, which Miranda did. At some point, we took a taxi somewhere. We stopped off at the apartment on Central Park West where her mother and two younger half sisters lived. This was not the kind of much-desired Upper West Side building that has hallways exactly like the hallways of an insane asylum. This was tufted wealth. Park views and a wraparound terrace. Many rooms, pearl gray and ample. Miranda was an heiress! At any rate, she was the daughter of an heiress. Her mother was an actress and a writer who gave off a brainy, hippie serenity—I loved her instantly.

What else happened that day?

Miranda bought something gimcrack off a table on the street—a brightly colored set of bracelets or something like that. She had an audition later. Perhaps she'd meet a few friends after that, near her own apartment in an East Seventies high-rise. Nothing much, really. It was a loose day, open to improvisation.

That was the key, really, the impromptu quality of it, and the only way I can convey the impact it had on me is to stress what an exclusive product I still was of sluggish years in the suburbs and wonkish ones in the Ivy League. In Miranda's bopping life, there was a forecast of what it might be to be young, in New York, in the arts. The freedom of the city summed up in the person of a lively young woman.

Patti and I did, triumphantly, find a too-small apartment, on Broadway in the Fifties, in the building full of call girls. After the anxiety of searching for a place, an endless dispiriting process, and the move, during which our cat went missing for eight hours (he was hiding in the radiator), a day came when everything was open-ended and exhilarating, a lovely September day. I was looking forward to unpacking boxes and after that—who knows? Something joyous would present itself.

We were drinking coffee. I was on the sofa, Patti on the other side of the room, reading the *Times*. She looked up at me from the paper, quite slowly. She said nothing.

"What?" I finally asked, impatient, as I often was.

Miranda had died. My name and the name of my play were in the obit. The cause of death was—well, what was the cause of death?

There was a viewing at Frank Campbell's that night. Patti helped me buy a tie. I'd never seen an open casket before and was surprised that it was not upsetting. The corpse, prettily made up and tidily arranged, was just unreal enough as not to stir the imagination. Word was, she had died of a violent asthma attack.

Several days later, there was a casual gathering at her mother's apartment, friends sharing memories. We sat on scattered chairs and sofas and hassocks and on the floor. I was moved by how young Miranda's friends were, though now I would consider them my exact contemporaries.

There was also an old woman there.

Not merely old: anachronistic, imperious in a straight-back chair. Either she leaned forward on a cane or my memory has assigned a cane to her. She was the only one in the room dressed in mourning. In the eighties, a room in Manhattan where only one person was wearing black made an unusual picture.

After some awkwardness, the memories flowed. Steamed vegetables! Miranda always ate steamed vegetables. (In fact, they were what she had ordered at our lunch.) The young men in the room had all had crushes on her. ("Really?" her mother asked charmingly, scanning us. "All of you?") She—well, I don't remember much more, but it was like that.

The weightless reminiscing went on for quite some time and it appeased something in the young people—something dumbfounded and outraged, the sense of not knowing how to proceed here in terra incognita, this land of tragic newness.

Then the old woman announced that she would like to speak. Her voice was cracked, rumbling, and she had a German accent—it was one of those ancient voices that make the voices of the young sound as shamefully inconsequential as they are.

"Everyone has been speaking so lightly," she intoned, "of steamed vegetables and such things. Now I would like to describe discovering my darling's dead body. May I?"

Silence.

"As you wish," Miranda's mother said, very quietly.

As the old woman spoke, I found myself watching Miranda's mother. Her eyes were downcast and her mouth was working in a relentless, particular way, in near-synch with the old woman's monologue. It occurred to me that she was trying to swallow her mother's words before anyone could hear them, and that this was an old habit. The descriptions Miranda's grandmother gave were Jacobean and delivered with sincere yet operatic emotion. I believe that all of us in the room were trying to be respectfully still and deafen ourselves to her, but one detail made me come to attention. It was when the old woman said she saw her "darling's body lying in a pool of blood."

I couldn't figure out what a pool of blood had to do with an asthma attack.

The evening was gotten through somehow and I saw Miranda's mother a few times after that. She was such a nice woman and the most terrible thing had happened to her. That was all I could make of the situation; nothing deeper or even slicker came to mind.

Fourteen years later, I was starting a workshop of a new play. First-rehearsal introductions were made. The stage manager was a young woman with a familiar name. I looked at her quizzically; she gave me a look back that indicated she would have something to say later. At the first break, she told me that, yes, she was Miranda's little sister. This was the tiny, adorable red-haired girl who had cried so stormily that evening when we'd gathered and, upon being comforted, laughed heartbreakingly. Somehow she had turned out all right; there was a calm about her.

It hadn't come easily, she told me. The family had been

a mess for a while. They'd uprooted to L.A., swapping homes with a well-known acting couple famous for leaving a wake of chaos wherever they perched. The beautiful apartment, when they returned to it, was a shambles.

They got it in order. Eventually, they got everything in order.

I asked the question. What did Miranda die of, really?

She sighed; it was an old question for her. She didn't know, really. She thought it had been a bad interaction of two drugs. At least one of the drugs had been a prescription, the other may not have been recreational. But she knew little more than I did.

Seven years later, I don't remember why, I found myself on Miranda's Wikipedia page. There I learned that she'd been murdered. The truth of this claim was in dispute. It was perhaps nothing more than a viral rumor, long-standing and with two strains. In one, she had been beaten to death by an ex-boyfriend. The other maintained that a mentally unbalanced fan, under the misimpression that Miranda had snubbed him, snuck into her apartment and did the deed. I didn't know what to make of any of this. I found it distasteful that someone who was bored or malicious or overeager had taken the violent end of someone I had cared about and used it for entertainment. It was more distasteful that, at a distance of two decades, I might be among the entertained.

I decided the story was nonsense, a canard.

. . .

It would explain that pool of blood, though.

As it happened, I'd known a young woman who had been murdered, verifiably, a year or so before Miranda died. We'd acted in a play together during a lost year I spent as a PhD candidate at Harvard. After Harvard, I went to drama school, and during my last year there, I had a play produced in New York. I'd stayed at my parents' house on Long Island after the first preview, and when I came downstairs the next morning, my mother said, "What a terrible thing, this young woman stabbed on her roof." She got the name wrong but I figured out whom she meant.

It seems that the woman, Caroline, had come home late from the theater—she'd seen David Rabe's great play *Hurlyburly*—and gotten on the elevator with the (schizophrenic? drug-addled?) son of her building's super. He blocked her when she tried to get off at her floor and pushed the button to take them to the roof. There he attempted to rape her and, failing when she fought him off, stabbed her repeatedly.

I remember there was a great deal of controversy over her last sentence, spoken from her hospital bed: "I should have let him do it."

This was a time when it was considered perfectly kosher to chastise a murdered woman because her dying words had been politically less than just so.

Though I knew Caroline hardly at all, we had had one nice talk, when, rehearsal having gone quite late, I insisted on accompanying her to her dorm building.

Cambridge was a sympathetic place where students felt at ease, but bad things happened to women when they traveled alone in the city.

As far as I know, the question of Miranda's death has never been settled to anyone's satisfaction. If she had been murdered, wouldn't it have been investigated, pursued—known about, even if no culprit was ever found?

Then I think of the gothic grandmother and a slew of *Law & Order* plots assail me—rich families wielding their power to shut the law down because the murderer was one of their own. (Or to spare the little sisters the horror of the truth?)

Then again, it was probably a lie.

Miranda's death shocked because she was not the type to die—she was too much like us. Had she lived, I believe we would have been friends, at least for a while. On a single afternoon, she made me feel that life in the city could be off the cuff, and abundant. It hasn't turned out like that. It never does.

Dorie

Dorie was so proud when she called with the news. She'd found a vegetable recipe she liked! It was a recipe for cauliflower and its first six ingredients were cream, butter, Parmesan cheese, bacon, eggs, and Gruyère cheese.

She was, like most of the women of her generation that I've known, a disciple of Julia Child. I believe their feeling for Julia was akin to the worship expressed by all those guys in *The Manchurian Candidate* who, upon hearing the name of their leader, would glassily recite, "He's the warmest, most wonderful man I've ever known." Julia Child's byzantine recipes tortured those poor women. By the time one of them gave a dinner party, she'd be so exhausted her head would fall into the soup.

Even though Dorie still ate this way, she was not fat. She was short with a perfectly flat stomach, which we got to see when, struck by a sudden inspiration or remembering an explosively funny joke, she would dash from the women's dressing room to the men's, wearing nothing but black jeans and a bra. This leanness may have had something to do with the chain smoking, which she kept up after two cancer scares and one cancer bout. The smoking in turn might be the reason that at fifty-one she could play a well-preserved seventy-year-old in my play and no one was the wiser. She did an awfully good job and we became friends.

The friendship only got to last two years, and I question my role in it.

Dorie had been a young woman when I was a starry-eyed child, and I could mentally regress her to that time so successfully that it's possible the pictures I made of her obscured my view of the person whose company I was in, reducing her to a series of mnemonic cues—a symbol for a time I found romantic. This is extreme, but I wonder.

I remember her in bits. I don't recall the dailiness of the friendship, though we were always in touch. I remember facts, episodes. Qualities.

For instance: her tininess.

One year at the Emmys (she was nominated), Patty Duke, another tiny woman, said to her, "Where were you when I had that TV show?" On the TV show, Patty Duke had played identical twin cousins (don't question it). Dorie was often mistaken for Patty Duke. There was no percentage in this.

She had one of those Los Angeles acting careers, more successful than most. Recurring roles on TV series. Mothers and best friends. Small but meaty parts in movies. Employed often, capable of supporting herself, well respected. Not famous.

Once, there'd been reason to believe bigger things would happen for her. In her first movie—she'd gotten an "and introducing" credit!—she played Joanne Woodward's disappointingly chubby daughter. (As a very thin woman, she looked like a formerly plump woman.) She was a resentful daughter in that movie, sidelined by her mother's coldness and materialism.*

I suspect she had mother issues of her own—mother issues, father issues, sister issues, something. They manifested in a residue of personality, one I understood so well.

She would find sneaky ways to cut you down to size.

"Boy, does she respect you as a writer," she said of a friend who'd just seen our play—a bitter, unkind woman I'd known slightly for years. "What did she think of *this* play?" I was constrained to ask. Then Dorie's eyes got glittery and she dove into the bad news.

I didn't mind. I understood!

I understood because the Dorie pastiche I'd devised and doted on explained it all so thoroughly. She was Dorie the archetype and I could extend myself to her.

I knew all about the fat and glowering little-girl years. Those trips to Jones Beach, all chafing thighs and prickly heat. Taunting older sisters and butter-wouldn't-melt Old

---

*This was the seventies and all movie mothers were cold, except the Jewish ones, who were castrating.

Country aunts with their "Dahlink, so ya still like the per-taters?" The *ferbisseneh* mother with a voice like a serpent hissing out undermining assessments. Father brooding in the Naugahyde chair, stomach churning acids; his judgments. I understood the whole Jewish Long Island megillah, affluent and haunted and insane.

I also knew how she was a few years later, in her late teens and early twenties.

Haunchy in a miniskirt and shearling coat with collar fluff, thigh-high boots.

They were not lucky, those poignant, desirable women, to have come of age when the sexual revolution was in high gear but the women's movement hadn't yet kicked in.

They lacked a rationale to say no.

There were all these men of achievement everywhere. Older men with steel-wool tonsures, potbellies, pervasive tobacco stench, dressed in plaid suits and spin-art ties. Patiently, the men analyzed why the women were rebuffing their advances.

They were *daddy's girls*. They were *prisses*. They were hopelessly bourgeois, they needed to go back to Scarsdale and marry a gelding of a dentist named Bruce Epstein.

Thus demolished, the women would sleep with them after all and find it disgusting and cry or withdraw after. Then the rather revolting men, so consumed by amour propre they couldn't imagine that love of themselves was not a universal emotion, lifted their typewriter covers and wrote novels in which the women were depicted as insane bitches.

A single sentence would have rescued these women: *I really find you extremely unattractive.*

But no one would be allowed to utter this sentence for years.

The truth is, of course, that Dorie may not have suffered that kind of childhood or been misused by that kind of man.

We were friends for two years. She was warmhearted, I remember, clever, informed, verbally dextrous. She was always making up lyrics just for fun. The lyrics leaned rather too heavily on inversions. "Your mood so cheery / Is making me leery." We talked a lot, endlessly, on all sorts of subjects—recipes; the seventies; certain older men she'd dated; Bette Davis, whom she'd befriended. We squabbled a bit, never seriously. She remained fifty percent a type.

Dorie appeared twice in one play of mine—a farce—first in California, then in New York. Between the two productions, she had another cancer scare, this time not a false alarm. It was a rare cancer for which there was no standard treatment. As I understood it, the doctors called upon the procedures used to treat cancer of the most proximate organ. This worked, and a year later, she rented an Upper

West Side sublet—I went into every restaurant in the neighborhood to collect delivery menus for her—and took her place in our company. When, at first rehearsal, she walked exactly like Groucho Marx, the director drew me aside and said, "Tell me that Dorie is going to be able to do this play." I assured him she would and she made good on my promise. By first preview, she was homo erectus once more. Her voice could be gruff, but that's actors.

After we closed, she stayed on a while in the city, auditioned for plays, believed the next phase of her life had commenced. She traveled to Europe, then dreamed of another trip, this one along the spice route. She got a puppy and named him after a gay German man she had met in her travels who thought she was the bee's knees. She returned to L.A., had her house repainted. She was grateful to me; my play had changed her life.

In the spring of 2000, I was in a hotel room in California when I got a call from one of Dorie's friends. (I was rehearsing a new play at the same theater where we'd first done the farce.) The friend told me that Dorie had gone for a checkup; the news was bad, the worst. The cancer was back, she had six months. (They really do say "six months.")

Stunned, I muttered a few solemnly meaningless words, wanting off this call.

"Here," the friend said. "Talk to her."

The dying Dorie got on the phone. She sounded level, intrepid. She sounded like herself. I'd always liked the way she spoke. She had period diction. That accent is gone now—it started vanishing in the eighties. Watch a *Columbo* rerun and you'll know what I mean; it's a sound shared by the good and bad actresses alike. Not the fake British intonations that dominated the early talkies, but broad-voweled, classy. Dorie had the endearing Jewish-fancy variant.

I was useless on the phone—babbling, sentimental. Finally, she cried out, "Oh, this is too much!" and thrust the phone back at her friend.

Ileen, also, had been in the farce, and a quiet rivalry had developed between them—for my attention!

Actresses.

At the shiva, Ileen confided to Dorie's sisters that, some dozen years before, she herself had survived ovarian cancer, though she'd been certain she was going to die. Later, another actress told me she thought this had been inappropriate sharing, but I'm not so sure.

You try so hard to be helpful at these things and "I'm sorry your baby sister died" is a lousy conversation starter.

Five years later, Ileen died.

Ileen

I was certain she was going to be an ineradicable TV presence, one of those actors who feature in memories of childhood and years later people quiz one another as to what their names were.

Like those actors, she was endlessly useful and highly specific.

Physically ample, most of the time, with a leonine head. Even more than the body, it was the voice that marked her.

It had a friendly range, the sound she used for banter, a gusty alto with a nasal edge. From there, it dove down and widened and amplified into a sonorous baritone, which, when she was tired—or felt like it—lowered still further and fell back into her throat, approximating the radio sound effect called "the creaking door."

That valuable thing—a character actress.

She had the most extraordinary funeral, on what would have been her forty-fourth birthday. SRO in a very large chapel on the Upper West Side. Her lovely steadfast husband held the younger of their two adopted children in his arm and told us of how, that last night at the hospital, he'd whispered to her that it was all right, she could go, and when she finally did slip away, the radio, tuned to a classic pop station, started playing "I'll Be Seeing You." Many who attended the funeral were famous. Ileen had a talent for befriending; sometimes the talent bordered on mania. She brought people together. One of her eulogists described us mourners as belonging to the "commonwealth of Ileen," and it was true. When you knew her, you felt populated. Occasionally, the citizenry rebelled.

Wasn't this drive she had, this compulsion to be included, intrusive? At parties, small groups could snark. Leslie once was present when this was happening and said, "Ileen would never say these things about you." And she wouldn't. Most of us are saddened by our friends' accomplishments; Ileen gloried in them. You always knew the marvels being wrought by those around you because Ileen would report them to you in her sprightliest voice. She was honored to be hanging with such a distinguished group. When she was in a mood to show up too often, or hectically insist on organizing one party too many, the others bridled, Leslie believed, because Ileen was too nakedly displaying the mortal insecurities they suavely concealed. It snuck up on them. That was unnerving. You have to primp for a mirror. Was there something in her childhood that made her torque a little? Probably. This distinguishes her from exactly three people. Most of us have warped in more invidious ways.

I never felt this pressure from Ileen because my limits are strict and no one exceeds them. For me, her availability was all upside. She was smart and funny as hell. Once, bored, I was being obnoxious on the phone. "I'm going to call somebody better," she said. In the first play we did together, she was half of a hard-luck married couple, the Stempels. Actors, if you don't stop them in time, will refer to their "journey." Ileen decided that the Stempels had a "shlep." This is not making the point. You need to hear the delivery. On a hit sitcom, she had a running role in which she gave one of the greatest deadpan performances ever. She might have repeated that, with variations, for decades. It would have served her.

When she started having the strange, persistent symptoms, a troubled gut, the doctor told her, "This isn't going to kill you."

Ah, well.

Two things happened to me in the year after Ileen died.

First, after a season in which I'd had five plays in overlapping productions, there was nothing coming up. I had time.

Second, I became rich.

Let me clarify that. By the standards of the rich, I was not rich. I was a pauper. But, very quickly, from a revival starring an earth-shaking movie star, I earned enough money to live for several years before I'd have to start worrying about money again.

And I found I had nothing to do.

This was more perplexing than it sounds. There'd been other years when work wasn't imminent and this year, even without a production coming up, I was still writing. But never before had I had such a strong feeling of unappointed time—evacuated time. I couldn't figure it out. How had I filled my days?

I asked Leslie: "What was I doing in those years that I wasn't doing now?"

"Were you talking to Ileen?" she said.

That was it. I was talking to Ileen.

Jill

The reason I wrote my worst play was that the apocalypse was coming.

The form it was set to take was the Republican National Convention of 2004. That this event would trigger End Times was so obvious to me I couldn't believe it was being allowed to go forward, and this decision I felt represented a kind of grand capitulation—roll-over-and-die on a cosmic scale. As a result, I was having the kind of thing the late actor Anthony Holland, in explaining why he was withdrawing from a play, had called a "nervous breakdown-ette." I didn't know how to play my part in the oncoming cataclysm. At every moment I believed I was about to be ejected into chaos and was in a state of electric unreadiness. After 9/11, Homeland Security put out a public-service scare video, advising us to have a go-bag to hand. It ended with a creepy kid staring us down and saying, "Get ready, people." Apparently, the powers-that-be thought their most effective pitchman was Piggy from *Lord of the Flies*. I resented Piggy and refused to prepare the bag, or prepare at all. Hence, my nervous breakdown-ette. The only thing that calmed me was writing. Not merely engagement with a writing project; the physical act of writing itself.

So I wrote.

Fortunately, when the terror moved in, I'd already been working on three linked one-acts that were saturated with dread. As I was nearing the end of them, a long play I had been pondering—writing at, dodging—came together, one night as I lay in bed, trying to bring on sleep. This happens sometimes: an idea simply drops in. The day after I completed the one-acts, I applied myself to the long play. Writing it was a pleasure and a sedative and the work flowed.

Flowed too freely. I was about to finish and my mental condition was unimproved.

I finished.

I needed to start another play.

I didn't have an idea for another play.

I made one up.

On the floor, watching TV, I plotted the play I would begin the next morning.

Lacking an idea, I created a pretext.

I had, as a template for a couple of earlier plays, made ironic use of Broadway commercial comedies—those featherweight plays with airborne titles like *Sunday in New York* and *Come Blow Your Horn*.

What if I wrote one straight-up?

That's what I would do.

On the face of it, it was a good choice. I knew the form well, and in adopting it, I nullified the tricky question of substance. There would be no substance.

The next morning, I got to work. I worked steadily for three days, chronologically, page one to page the last, and at six in the evening of the third day typed THE END.

Two days later, after corrections and copies, I sent the play off to the theater in California.

Three days after that, they chose it for their spring mainstage production.

Eight days had elapsed between my decision to write a play and the addition of that play to the schedule of a major regional theater.

For a time, this waylaid judgment. If a play could travel from zero to contract in barely more than a week, perhaps there was some kind of pixie dust about it.

I will say this in the play's defense: if you read it on a plane, you thought it was hilarious. I know this for a fact. Patti read it on a plane and thought it was hilarious. The forces that fueled the writing, terror and adrenaline, gave the play a speedy, jokey momentum and many of the jokes were strong. The two-dimensionality of reading—the look of words on a page, the comic timing implicit in negative space—was also helpful. The play might have worked well as a humor piece in a magazine—something intended as a time-passer as you waited to do something else—as opposed to a play in a theater, for which you set other activities aside.

We'd assembled some very good actors for the California production, alas. Good actors don't flesh out thin characters; they expose them. I was steadily depressed all through rehearsal, and before the play started on opening night, as people I respected greeted me outside the theater, I found myself recommending other ways they might spend their evening.

Anyway, it opened. I hightailed it out of there the next day.

That should have been that. And it would have been, had I been high-minded and solvent. I was neither, and somehow my agent managed to persuade an excellent producer with whom I'd worked happily twice before to present my three-day wonder on Broadway. In addition, he hooked the play up with a director who's one of the smartest people I know. Very smart people's opinions of art products should be taken with a grain of salt. Often they believe that because a play or poem or novel has sprung fascinating thoughts in them, it is itself of high value. It isn't. They're just interesting people.

The director announced that my play was modern Molière, I said great, and off we went.

A new batch of excellent actors, plus a couple of excellent holdovers, and I was depressed all over again.

Except now there was Jill.

. . .

After she had (unbelievably) accepted our offer of the role, the casting director, on his way out of the room to start dickering with her agent about contract details, paused, turned to us, and said, "She was an *enormous* movie star."

This was not a "sic transit gloria mundi" observation. Nor was it a reminder. We all were well aware of the vastness of the cultural space she'd once occupied. The casting director was offering a tribute. Our little skit had netted someone who *mattered*.

After Jill died, I told someone that she was the least disappointing friend I'd ever had. Another friend got quite chesty about that.

Let me be clear:

I didn't mean that everyone else had let me down, only that Jill had had the greatest *potential* to disappoint because she'd had the biggest buildup—a quarter century long.

She was the movie star of my youth, during the most agreeable era of American movie stardom, when the national craze for getting real had trickled up to the studios, which, for the first time in their glossy history, were valorizing regular people in large numbers. This could be taken to ludicrous extremes (one year, Elliott Gould was the biggest star in film), and Jill could hardly be called ordinary. There was no question that she was better than you—better-looking than you, smarter, more vital, more endearing—better than you in every way. But she was better than you the way your most glamorous friend is. She had flaws. Pauline Kael thought her pretty but blurry. She was believable. More important, she was *nice*.

She was lucky to peak in a time when the word "icon" referred to trinkets you bought in a Christian supply store, or she would have been a feminist one. It was a particular sliver of feminism: affluent white women on a quest for self-actualization.

This quest dovetailed with a broader one. The word "yuppie" had not yet been coined, but the middle-class hippies had made their transition and were looking for ways to approve of themselves while leading the lives of safe and seamless pleasure and egotism for which they'd originally been groomed. The movie that made Jill a star—a movie that still stands up chiefly because of her performance—fit the bill. It was about a serious topic—a woman in transition—thus was a serious film, yet it went down easy as whipped cream. You knew you were not wasting your time as you watched it, yet you weren't having a difficult time. It was the same irresistible combination that marked Woody Allen's best films, and there was a promise in it, a hint that all life could be like this—painless, lustrous, and above reproach. Right now, that sensibility is perhaps best expressed by the kind of enlightened corporatism practiced by Bill Gates and Starbucks and Ben & Jerry's. Yes, you think, yes, yes, absolutely, yes . . . but . . .

There's always been something eerie about this airtight perfection, this virtue that costs nothing, yet when the theory was still forming, its yield could be exhilarating. In the sixties and early seventies, if you went to a movie, you really couldn't eat after. Once you'd seen twenty-year-old junkie Susan Sarandon accidentally shot dead by her white-collar father, all you were good for was an aspirin.

When you watched Jill lugging an oversized painting through the streets of a newly burgeoning Soho in a state of dazed bliss, you wanted to dance.

She was the heroine the time was ready for, one who had carryover traits from the romantic ingenues Jane Fonda had played a decade earlier. (Startlingly, and, perhaps, unintentionally, the title graphics of Jill's breakthrough film underscore the point—they're the same cake-frosting cursive that was used for movies like *Any Wednesday*.)

Like Fonda's characters, Jill's are ditzy and scrumptious and yearning to be loved. The difference is that where Fonda is ditzy from feeblemindedness, Jill is coping with too many thoughts, sharp brain and tender heart striving for an elusive balance. Fonda is subjugated in love. Jill, when she finds the right guy, experiences love as an aspect of liberation.

A strong heroine was not a new idea, of course. She had been a feature of high comedies of the thirties and forties like *The Awful Truth*. In those, that strength came off as an aristocratic prerogative. The Jill heroine helped democratize the privilege and establish it as a right.

When she died, the comment threads were heartbroken. Women—strangers—wrote, "This one hurts." For these women, her death didn't represent the loss of youth, but of tentative, blooming middle age, the dream of a second chance.

The stunning—crushing—truth was that the woman the strangers lost was very much the one her friends lost.

I told her once, fully aware of the throwback savor of the phrase, that she was an adorable chucklehead.

She enjoyed that, its period quality, the oblique reference to her movie star days.

She gave up the movie stardom when it was still robust, to have and care for her kids. ("That's what I *tell* people," I once heard her say.) She never seemed to regret this. She kept her hand in—one or two well-paying TV movies a year. When she did my play, it was a return to theater in New York after an absence of decades, at the beginning of a season in which she'd do play after play—four of them in all. She was ubiquitous that season.

She was lovely to work with, though very concentrated, not an immediate pal. At breaks, she took out a giant bento box of pills, from which she sampled as though it were a smorgasbord table. She'd give a tour, if you asked—all sorts of supplements, holistic stuff, immune boosters, I don't know what. Daffy.

We became friends all at once one night when we found ourselves together at a surprise birthday party on a boat that toured the Hudson. It was a sweltering night and the lobster was tough, but we talked, a little formally at first—we were both polite, by nature—then more freely, and that was that.

I had no idea what she saw in me, but I didn't question it. She would come to my apartment for dinner, although looking at her, you imagined she didn't eat. Her disciplined body was taut, allergic to fat. In fact, she ate only one meal a day but she ate it like a cheetah. When I feared I'd undercooked a chicken breast (I always think I've undercooked the chicken), Jill snatched it up and consumed it in a single gulp. That was nothing; she boasted of having eating chicken livers raw. This svelte, elegant woman was a voluptuary who could sensualize anything—even the accoutrements of illness. Once, in preparation for a medical procedure, I had to stop using analgesics. When it was over, I mentioned that I could take Advil again. In her Dark Lady voice—which was one of her voices—she purred, "You can take A-a-advil again." You'd have thought it was foie gras.

We'd been friends about a year when she confided that all that mysterious coughing she'd been doing lately was not so mysterious. It was a recurrence of the leukemia she'd had full-bore twenty years earlier. There'd been one or two episodes, subsequently. This was bigger. That bento box had nothing to do with her being an adorable chucklehead.

She asked me to tell Leslie, who'd also been in my terrible play and also become her close friend. Leslie is emotional. I'm drier. It would be easier for her to get the news from me.

Near the end of her life, Jill and I were sharing a cab when she described her visit with a palliative care doctor.

Tanatalizing as Scheherazade, he'd asked, "Do you want to know how you're going to die?"

"Yes!" she'd cried. And as she relived the moment, her eyes were dancing.

"I thought that was so amazing," I said to Leslie, "how easily she talked about her death—and she talked about it all the time."

"She didn't with me," said Leslie.

Well, of course not.

Some people say the same things in the same way to everyone they know. You think you're conversing with them; you're merely partnering their monologue. Jill had conversations that *pertained* to the person she was talking to. There was no double-dealing in this. She *saw* us.

In the years between the diagnosis and her death, she had an exhausting schedule. She was on a TV series, made a couple of movies, socialized constantly.

She continued to come to dinner at my apartment. I

(this is embarrassing) had replaced the original cast albums of my childhood with CD versions. I was able to get all the way through each of the ones I'd removed from the shrink-wrap at least once (except *Mame*). After dinner, Jill would lie on my sofa and listen to the albums of the shows she had seen as a child, *Fanny* and shows like that. She would describe the staging of dance numbers. On certain songs, she would close her eyes, prop her folded hands against her stomach, and sing along. She prepared very carefully for high notes, loosening her jaw, lifting her palate, and taking a measured breath; she never missed. There was a pentimento quality to this.

She had been in Broadway musicals herself, in the seventies—the glowing ingenue star of *The Rothschilds* and *Pippin.*

The movie career that followed was much vaster. By the time we met, *Entertainment Weekly* had named her one of the twenty-five greatest actresses in film history.

And here she was on my sofa—my sofa!—singing along to cast albums, like a stage-struck kid dreaming of joining these (mostly forgotten) stars in the Broadway empyrean. I felt as though I was watching a montage, one of those late-in-the-movie surveys of a whole life.

She spent her last year or so busily interfering in the lives of everyone she loved. I was ordered to exercise (I did, too, before I busted my Achilles tendon). She tracked Leslie's progress at finding a place she could live in the city after two decades in New Jersey, demanding an update even from her hospital bed on a very uncomfortable afternoon. Her daughter she was hoping to get married, a son, just out of college, to accelerate to some firm position in life that no one just out of college has any business occupying. One of her friends was charged with finding her husband his next wife. She was like a moribund Emma Woodhouse, dealing out happy endings. Only we weren't ending.

The last time I saw her was toward the end of her final hospital stay. Visitation was limited, so I pretended that I'd been in a cab on the West Side Highway heading to see a friend when the thought popped into my head, What the hell, why not go another mile and see if they'll let me look in on Jill? I was allowed in after a little wait. She had a room in the fancy wing—the only visibly fancy thing about it was a baby grand piano in the waiting area that no one ever seemed to play—and when I came in, she was searching her lunch tray for the kobe beef she thought she'd ordered. I looked at her lunch card and pointed out that she hadn't checked off the beef. She was disappointed. She didn't have an appetite, but she was an epicurean without an appetite.

Her family was there and the mood was almost festive. The kids were spirited—there was a lot of everyday talk about their schedules and logistics—and her husband was very taken up with how much he hated the acclaimed memoir of a rock star he'd loathed for forty years. Somewhere in the middle of this, Jill decided to share a recipe with me, I have no idea why. She couldn't remember the word for a cracked-open chicken. "Butterflied," I said. She shook that off impatiently. "Well, that's what it *is*," I muttered. She started listing ingredients. Suddenly I remembered the word she'd been searching for: "Spatchcocked!" This pleased her and she started the ingredient list from the top. It included mustard, garlic, lemon, rosemary, and thyme. I said good-bye. A few days later, she died gazing at the mountain view through the window of her den in Connecticut.

Both Jill and Ileen had doubles.

Jill's was spotted by Leslie and her husband, Sam, on the Upper West Side several times in the weeks after Jill's death. She had the same skewed beauty, definite walk. That sense, on a city street, that she belonged. That, really, she was the flawed, kind, superior reason for having city streets.

As mysteriously as the double appeared, she vanished.

Ileen's double was seen only by me and I was aware of her long before she became a double.

She was a pleasant woman who lived in the same entryway I did in London Terrace. I would see her in the elevator, we would nod cordially. I still don't know her name. It never occurred to me that she favored Ileen.

In the last phase of Ileen's illness, when we all thought she was well, she lost weight, eventually becoming quite thin. Wonderfully thin. Ileen, who had always been so full of energy, so eager to fit in, finally had a body to match her spirit. She wore these sort of capri pants and cute nubbly sweaters. It was a lovely time. Then there was something about the blood-brain barrier and we were all making hasty visits to the hospital, where she was a skeleton, shaking and blind and unaware of us.

But in the weeks before that, I saw that neighbor on the street (I was now living in my new apartment) and she was Ileen's twin. I'd never known a resemblance like it.

I didn't see her again for two years. Then I was in the diner and she walked in.

I gasped.

It must have been a subtle gasp because the friend I was with didn't seem to notice it.

He had known Ileen. I thought of pointing her double out to him but I didn't. That swiveled-head gawk is rude.

Besides, some ghosts are not for sharing.

[THINGS ARE LOOKING UP, MAYBE; AND BACK]

Opinions

I have recently given up having opinions and it's going very well; thank you for asking. You don't go cold turkey on something unless it's become bad for you, and before the renunciation, I opined relentlessly and about everything: plays, books, people, food, weather. Between experiencing a thing and registering an opinion of it, I allowed virtually no time to elapse. At a certain point, I found myself weighing in about things *before* I experienced them. From there, I found myself inveighing against events that had been announced for some vague date in the distant future, then against projects that had not been announced but that I suspected might be in the works.

The truth about opinions is that they are seldom impartial. In fact, they are seldom opinions. They are many other things: attempts to equalize, preemptive strikes, psychological hedges. In the early eighties, one was constantly reading reviews extolling books of short stories written by young writers on the topic of family dysfunction. The reviews themselves had been written by young writers who were about to publish books of short stories on the topic of family dysfunction. In these cases, opinion was designed to foster a *climate* of opinion. Unless an opinion is self-perpetuating, it is of little use and leaves a sour, charred aftertaste. It also becomes a mirror of the very inadequacies it had been proffered to disguise.

Giving up opinions is a process, and you can go overboard with it. Judgments are opinions that have been tested and retested, provisionally discarded and irresistibly reinstated, and they are, of course, of great value, the ensign of maturity. How do you maintain judgments—well-vetted opinions—if you refuse to have opinions to begin with? I'm still working that out.

It's also foolish to try to blunt your responsiveness to the world as a way to prevent opining. When I say that I've given up having opinions, what I mean is that I am trying to respect the distance between response and verdict, to stop mistaking my feelings about a thing for the objective value of that thing.

What makes this difficult is that it requires modesty, and modesty is a form of self-concealment. I prefer that to self-expression, which, if I were still having opinions, I would consider overrated.

Nuptials

Emma got married because I canceled brunch.

I honestly didn't think I would be canceling this time, though cancelation is what I do. Theologically I'm atheist, but I'm a holy fool when it comes to my bronchitis. No matter how often it's been demonstrated otherwise, I continue to believe that the racketing, convulsive phase will pass in a day or two and virtually every date I make contains the sentence "I'm *sure* I'll be better by then."

Well, I never am better by then, though I push it to the last minute. We were very much looking forward to this brunch because it was to be on a Friday. Emma's SOP is to work six days a week—she especially loves the prayerful conditions of her office on Saturdays, when she can be alone with the staid machinery hum—but this was her vacation, she wanted to express her freedom, and for people as obedient as we are, brunch on a Friday counts as devil-may-care.

I'd tendered my apologies and hit the couch where I

watched a marathon of whatever—*The Real Housewives of Ulan Bator*, I think it was—and after nine or so episodes, I turned on my computer. There was an e-mail from Emma with an attachment. The attachment was a photograph of Emma and her girlfriend, Louise, brandishing a certificate of some kind. The caption read *Louise, our marriage license, and I.*

I replied:

?

I didn't know what to make of it. Though Emma is not without a sense of humor, it's close to the vest, in the Jewish-ironical mode that we love and practice in a conscientious spirit of preservation. What I mean to say is she is no kind of joker, so little a prankster that no prank has ever been played *against* her; the sporty types know to lay off.

What had happened? Had marriage ever even been discussed between Emma and Louise? Not to my knowledge, though same-sex marriage had been legal only days at the time of the brunch cancelation, so it's possible they had discussed it, long ago, in the misty, theoretical way you talk about what is safely impossible. I don't know. If I'd heard about it, I'd forgotten. Certainly it had not been a front-burner issue. Certainly not for *Emma*.

What do I say about Emma's history in the closet?

If I tell you she had been closeted about her sexuality,

it's only fair to add that she was closeted, too, about her salary, her dietary habits, her preference in clothes, her favorite color, and her true feelings about her friends. That is to say that she was shy. Diffident. For a decade or so she'd worked with therapists who had tried to abolish her shyness and replace it with shame. Once she'd finally twigged to what they were doing and fired her last preposterous shrink, she improved. The shame was, I'd say, mostly gone (had it been rooted in her sexuality? Isn't it always?) but the shyness remained, though with abatements.

I don't mean to suggest she was ever a shrinking violet. She didn't wish to have no impact. It was more, I think, that she would have preferred to be incorporeal. You picked up on this. Sometimes, meaning to compliment her on how pretty she looked that day, I found myself rerouting the praise to express how "professionally excellent" she appeared.

Professional excellence was her defining characteristic, her shining aim, and her steely underpinning. She was willful as a tiger. She didn't fear poverty or illness or bad neighborhoods. What terrified her was the possibility of making a mistake. She saw error as a dissolvent; think Margaret Hamilton in *The Wizard of Oz* (I dislike that movie but the image serves). In Emma's mind, an archive of achievement couldn't offset a single small error. She not only avoided making mistakes, she avoided correctnesses that might be *taken* for mistakes.

I'm with her on this.

For both of us, the word "banal" is a particular hobgoblin. The preferred pronunciation of banal is the intuitive one, the way people usually pronounce it the first time they encounter it—BAY-nal—but sophisticates invariably choose the secondary pronunciation ba-NAHL. What would someone like William F. Buckley have done with BAY-nal? But he could ooze his way through ba-NAAAHL with the full oily force of his personality and win praise for it. In contrast, if you say BAY-nal in public, you likely will be incorrectly corrected, which means you have to correct your corrector. And that gives you a certain kind of reputation. You're thought a martinet or a priss. Emma and I choose to say "commonplace" or "mundane" when we'd like to say "banal," to avoid complications, and we feel the loss.

About a minute after I'd sent my question mark, the phone rang.

"So you saw my e-mail."

"Yes. What was that? I don't understand."

"We got our marriage license."

". . . Really?"

"Yes!"

"*Why?*"

That wasn't meant the way it sounded. I meant: "Why *now?*" I meant: "How did it happen?" I meant: "How did it happen to *you?*" I meant: "How good!" I meant everything but to negate, which was the only thing I *did* do.

"I mean . . . how?"

She explained and still it didn't make any sense to me. When I'd canceled, she faced two empty hours. She doesn't like time that is not earmarked. She could have done some homework but this was her vacation, dammit! Just then, Louise wandered into the room, stroking a cat. They'd lived together for nine years and got along well and Louise looked so kind and fetching stroking the cat that Emma heard herself say, "Rich canceled brunch. Do you want to go downtown and pick up a marriage license?"

Louise thought for a moment. "I'm getting my hair cut at two."

"We'll be back by two," Emma assured her.

And so they'd headed to City Hall. The fact of marriage was preceding the thought of marriage, and why not?

I have made reference to Emma's doggedness.

When, a week later, an e-mail blast went out advising us to save the date and including the venue and the time, I was not surprised. Once posited, the thing had taken on immanent force, and Emma's attention to detail made things happen that couldn't happen, that don't happen.

Because *Emma wanted it.*

I can't tell you how unbelievable that is.

We knew each other in high school, lost track during college, met up again ten years later at a street corner, resumed. In the interim, we'd stopped lying in a partial way and, with each other, stopped lying entirely. For all her taciturnity, I know things about her, learned in the period of reunion, that startle me now because, since they were revealed, we've both become discreet again.

I know about her coming out to her mother in a letter, her mother's initial response (heartbreaking: *Thank God your father's dead!*) and her mother's subsequent response (lovely). I know that the first time she slept with a woman it was with a Sullivanian, and that the Sullivanians are a sect or a cult whose philosophy, as it's been described to me, is to constantly have sex in sprawling prewar apartments on the Upper West Side. Good as any, I guess.

Because of her shyness—her quality of retreat—each advance in her life has been celebratory. When she found a girlfriend, it was a triumph. When they moved in together, it was another triumph. Before that, when she'd stopped with the shrinks and become happy, we were all ecstatic. Still, I never expected *this*.

I sometimes wonder what it was like to be born into the Civil War era and live to see the advent of the flapper. Change is incremental yet *so many* increments? I'm not sure the distance we've come since Emma's and my childhood is much less monumental.

Think of that moment in the movie of my elementary school years *Valley of the Dolls*, when Sharon Tate delivers the beautifully tooled line, "You know how bitchy fags can be."

And she was the one we were supposed to like!

Jacqueline Susann wrote that line. Who were Jacqueline Susann's friends, anyway? I know that a renowned gay critic was one of them, and she's reputed to have had close friendships with many other gay men and women as well. This didn't stop her from writing "You know how bitchy fags can be," and perhaps there was no sense of division. The culture was the culture, after all; you fed it what it asked for.

Things, of course, had gotten better since *Valley of the Dolls*, more sensitive. But marriage? For most of our lives, it was inconceivable, beyond wanting.

I had, briefly, been of two minds about it myself, as recently as a couple of election cycles ago.

This was when it seemed possible that John Kerry would beat George W. Bush in the presidential election, at a time when many of us thought that George W. Bush was a kind of walking existential threat.

Toward the end of that election, when hope still stirred, there was a concentrated push on the issue of same-sex marriage. It "dominated the conversation," as talking heads say during elections, and when Bush was reelected, the consensus was that it was "values" issues that pushed him over. For a while, it was thought that that referred to the specter of same-sex marriage, which had intruded so forcefully, so noisily, into the campaign.

When this was still the belief, I met an actor, gay and smart, and we found ourselves standing on a street corner having a very pissed-off conversation about how "our own" had contributed to fucking up the election. Rights are rights, but there has to be a world to exercise them in, we agreed, and ousting Bush had been the sine qua non of planetary continuance. Of course it was an outrageous injustice that gays couldn't marry. Be strategic. Prioritize results. *Wait two weeks for the better one to get elected.* We spoke of the wisdom of Machiavelli and the perversity of self-scuppering grandstands.

Later it came out that the idea that gay marriage influenced the election was a misreading of the data; that wasn't the values issue that mattered to people. I didn't see the actor again but I'm sure, if I had, there would have been a sequel to our conversation and it would have been chastened.

In those days, people were still expressing a range of views. On an episode of her show *My Life on the D-List*, gay advocate Kathy Griffin ran into gay comedian Mario Cantone on an island somewhere and they confided, in whispers, that they weren't so keen on the idea of legalizing gay marriage because, as Kathy put it, "I don't think *straight* marriage should be legal."

There's that. To many, marriage is such a poisonous institution that to extend its franchise feels about as enlightened as those NRA prescriptions to arm *everybody.*

Another niggling concern (ambivalent is my version of gung ho; healthy people, feel free to skip this part): Back—minutes ago—when gay lives were denied access to the mainstream, they served (involuntarily) as a critique of it.

Now many of us marry and reproduce and live in the suburbs and discuss golf over dinner and rather resemble the
people who once shunned us. Rights and entitlements sap
oppositional energy. On that blessed, none-too-imminent
day when the last barriers fall, will some portion of the
critical faculty survive? Or will we all be discussing golf?
The gains are everything, non-negotiable; what may be
lost deserves a mention. I can find a cloud to fit any silver
lining.

But enough! Marriage is here, it's queer, we're all going
to be buying a lot more blenders.

Emma and Louise's wedding was set for ten on a Sunday
morning. Labor Day weekend. You book what you can book.

The room was in an old brownstone on one of those half
streets in Greenwich Village that still have cobblestones
and that even Google Maps has trouble finding. You walked
up two flights of an old narrow staircase with treads so
steeply warped that each step bids to feed you to the previ-
ous step. It was like a building at college and it was lovely.

I was not especially well dressed. I have a very nice
suit that I wear only to awards shows, which is to say I've
worn it once, but the hour and the brides assured me that
formality was not necessary, so I ended up, in my sport
jacket, being the most underdressed one there until one
of Emma's friends arrived late, in shirtsleeves, and sat on
the floor and spun like a top.

It was a Jewish wedding—there was a chuppa and a

rabbi. The rabbi was gay and made a speech about himself. What an honor it was for *him* to be there, how moving it was to *him*—some people are always the subject. When he finally noticed the brides, things picked up.

First of all, they looked great. Though they're attractive women, Emma usually chooses to come off professional, Louise bohemian, and neither of them puts a premium on glam. For the wedding they'd hired a makeup artist who was not one of those the-more-the-merrier types. She knew how to emphasize best features. The women were elegant and pretty and, in their beautiful cocktail-style dresses— God help me for this—hot.

The ceremony was more or less traditional except for one segment when Emma—retiring Emma!—turned to us and explained how this extraordinary event had come to be. She told us how mesmerized she'd been by recent events. She spoke at length about obsessively visiting the website of SCOTUS to read about DOMA—I'm willing to wager that never before had a wedding toast been so littered with acronyms—and for a time this wedding seemed as much political statement as intimate avowal. But the politics were filled with romance.

Everyone was so happy for them—this is trite, only there was something about the number and types of people who were being happy. There was Emma's mother, very sharp and calm and glowing like the mother of the bride. There were friends of various ages. Middle-aged people, self-conscious about how *natural* their happiness for them was. There were Orthodox Jews who were happy for them and even one or two conservative Christians who were happy for them—philosophies were in crisis but good will prevailed. Nicest of all were the little kids—nieces and nephews, ring bearers and flower girls—who were happy for them and thought nothing of it. After the ceremony, because it was still so early, a breakfast buffet was served and the party took on some of the character of the kind of party they have at the VFW, full of coffee urns and sausages. I got to talk to Louise's nice sister and Emma's gorgeous neurologist. There were one or two eccentric children and pleasant neighbors I knew from Emma's winter gatherings and I stayed a good long while, then was among the first to leave, as I usually am.

Even in the thick of situations, and very happy about it, I don't generally feel a part of things. I have lots of friends and acquaintances who count on me to lend a sympathetic ear and give good counsel, but when I bother having a picture of myself, it resembles, funnily enough, the slanderous picture I used to delight in of the New York City traffic tsar Janette Sadik-Khan—someone alone in a room, studying a computer simulation of the real world and, based on these researches, issuing commands as to how the traffic should flow. As much as I'd enjoyed the party—as I enjoy most parties—in the cab after, I felt, as always, that I was heading back to freedom.

Yet even though I can never quite get over the idea that hell is a person being allowed to enter my apartment without knocking first, I'm happy that Emma's life has taken her where it has. Shy Emma. Private Emma. She isn't different at heart, thank God, yet she's come such a distance. The change has been incremental but *so many* increments.

Byrne the Witch:
My Radical Youth

Good news! My murderous friend's murderousness is in remission. This has been going on for a while now: that roving look is gone and I don't wake in the night fearing his whereabouts and intentions. His drinking has lessened, too, is normal, and he's laid off the cryptic remarks, so I'm going to name him. I'm going to call him Jason, which is a *nom de livre.*

I suspect I've given the impression that Jason and I have a friendship based in extremity. We seem to meet only when he's gloomy or lethal or mad and my role is to temporize with him. It's not like that, really.

Jason and I became friends because he's one of the few men I know who consider conversation an event. Most men—all kinds of men: straight, gay, neuter—see discussion as a more or less bitter way station on the path to personal gain. It's like the compulsories in the Olympics: all those dreary figure-eights, but you have to do them to get what you want.

He and I talk about most things, though not about everything. We never discuss, for instance, who's secretly sleeping with whom, no matter how explosive that information is deemed to be. Make of this what you will, that sort of thing holds no interest for us.

We will discuss cultural effluvia—Twitter wars, TV reality crap—and we'll discuss other things that everyone discusses: recipes and that sort of topic.

We spend a lot of time talking about politics. *Talking* about politics is about all we ever do with politics, other than to vote on those odd occasions when we can remember where the polling place is, but we can talk with some heat. We get really riled up and in doing so consider ourselves highly moral. A minute later we're mortified that we felt virtuous because we'd said some words.

He and I belong to a sort of shadow generation—the much younger siblings of the engagé children of the sixties (though he is an only child). We had an example to look up to and we failed to emulate it, is the way we see it. There was a halo around those kids, created in large part by a popular culture industry that knew a great deal of money was to be mined from pandering to them. As we now know, much of that generation would shed its commitments and become greedy or remorseful, self-mocking or self-flacking, but their dissolution does little to make us feel better about our apathy. We knew ourselves to be apathetic even before we attained our majority. My high school newspaper was always publishing editorials decrying our apathy. Nobody ever read them (rim shot).

Jason and I were discussing this the other day, how we feel self-conscious when we try to be committed, to emulate the people we still respect: cussed city councilwomen and underpaid community organizers and the like. I reminded him of the time in the nineties when I joined a group on a bandstand in a rally that had been organized in support of the embattled National Endowment for the Arts. We were introduced as "some of the most talented artists in the country" and were seated in a block, facing the crowd, to express the strength of our solidarity. This was fictitious. Among us was this pissy bunch of self-identified provocateurs who kept loudly calling out slurs against the people whose side they were supposed to be on but who struck them as insufficiently something-or-other. Their jokes weren't funny and they weren't smart, only mean. And relentless. That was all it took to sour me for all time on rallies, and it shouldn't have been. It should have emboldened me. But I am not bold.

Usually, it's my role to appease Jason. That day he was trying to make *me* feel better, reassuring me that it was a good thing I was so politically abstemious. The gist of his argument was that I am not talented in those ways.

"First of all, there's your love of the concessive clause.

No one sticks a pin in his own argument the way you do. And that's how you *open*. By the time you let anyone in on what your point *is*, you've already trashed it. That doesn't work on a rostrum, buddy. Believe me, Che Guevara never said 'perhaps.' You're too non-doctrinaire! You're always seeing the other side. And no matter how wonkishly you've studied up on a subject, you still imagine you're under-informed. Somewhere, sometime, someone in the Czech Republic or someplace did something that proves you're full of shit. That doesn't get the signatures on the petition, my old. And you clam up in public. It's like you're physically disabled—you can't get the words out, you'd need hypnosis to stop stuttering. And, frankly, it's not worth undergoing treatment just so there can be another self-righteous *shrekker* at the hearing. Also, you have too elusive a relationship to the tangible. The world really isn't your priority. *Writing* about it is. You go places and do things not for the going and the doing but to bring back *nouns*. You come back and you get to write 'coal hauls' and 'hawsers' and 'oubliettes' and 'darning needle' and that's what gets you going, not realpolitik. It's your *temp*erament. Temperament is irre-ducible. The thing is, you're essentially a nostalgist. You can't agitate for the past, buddy. You can't polemicize Wee-juns or eating clubs or those lyrical afternoons at—*which* the fuck school did you go to—Princeton? Harvard? Yale? *All* of them, was it? That's ridiculous. The *problem* is your philosophy and your aesthetic contradict each other;

politically, you're this progressive, but you have a helpless attraction to the decorating schemes and the pullovers of the sorts of people who still say 'darky.' Also, you're intrinsically nonplural. You use the word 'we' only in the most restricted ways. There's never a hint of ideology about it or an edge of solidarity—if it's used to describe more than three people doing something prosaic, you think it doesn't fit you. What it all comes down to—and I know you hate this—is that you were *marinated* in the middle class. You are irre*med*iably bourgeois—which is to say, fear-driven. So *what*? Does it mean you're not a world historical figure? Of *course* you're not a world historical figure. Are you less useful, strictly speaking, than another sort of person? *Obv*iously you are. Big deal! You're *here*. The protoplasm can't be refunded. You make the best of the gifts you have. You're obsessed with the *sump* two blocks from where you grew up and the *tree*line on your property. Go in health. Don't worry about it. You're neither the problem *nor* the solution (*pace* the sixties). Just do what you do."

I was feeling a little abused by his compassion so, feebly, but in as snippy a voice as I could muster, I shot back, "What about *you*?"

"Me?" he said. "Jeez—puh!—*me*!"

We took leave of each other a few minutes later. Although not sorry to have had the talk, we were frustrated with our characters.

I was reminded of the conversation this morning when

I opened the *New York Times*—obituaries first, as always—and learned of the death of Jane Byrne, who, for a short time, had been the mayor of Chicago.

Before that, she'd held other prominent civic posts and in one of them, she'd earned the animus of a neighbor of mine who was a noted student revolutionary.

By "noted" I don't mean famous—he was never famous. His impressiveness derived from his having nabbed a high slot on Mayor Daley's enemies list, despite attending a college that more or less slept through the ructions of the sixties and early seventies.

He was universally acclaimed the nicest person in the neighborhood, as well as the brightest, and had been my babysitter and, later, something of a teacher to me. For example, in my early teens I thought of the sixties as an undifferentiated psychedelic mass. It was he who explained to me that a strong antagonism existed between the highly disciplined New Left and the hedonistic counterculture—albeit coming more from the left than the counterculture, who were always too stoned to stay mad at anything for very long.

I was twelve, I think, when he told me of a protest he'd spearheaded—or perhaps just attended—in which everybody had held signs—placards—that read "Byrne the Witch."

I, being a pretentious brownnose, said, "Why, that's—that's Shakespearean!"

And though I was only a child and of no account, he was

pleased by this bit of flattery. "It *is* Shakespearean," he whispered.

Once he had told me that within five years, the country (the United States) would be either socialist (good) or fascist (very bad). Absolutely no way around it.

When he said this, there was no maniacal glint in his eye, nothing supernatural or shifty about him. He was matter-of-fact. He was suburban. It was like hearing the Rapture being forecast by an accountant.

I was given to believe anything anyone told me if it was asserted with confidence. If two people asserted diametrically opposed ideas with equal confidence, my role was to have a nervous breakdown.

This was what was meant by "politics."

Life was barely tolerable for me in those days, but I imagined that any deviation from things as they were could only be cataclysmic. I started to worry about fascism the way people in high-crime neighborhoods worried about break-ins. Not if, but when.

This neighbor continued to drop by pretty regularly during school vacations, and it was always the same. He'd sit with the family, sipping tea, eating Entenmann's sour cream chip nut loaf, and predicting imminent social collapse in a pleasant tone of voice. He didn't cause panic in me—I was already a panicker—but his preachments reminded me that panicking was a good idea. And though he liked me, he couldn't see that the attitude of sangfroid I affected in his presence was a hoax, because he was a true believer.

Decades later, I dwell in a world of nuance and I no longer think that "Byrne the Witch" is Shakespearean.

And just for the record, if you advocate the immolation of heretics, who does that make you? Torquemada? A magistrate of Salem?

On the Other Hand . . .

Truly, I am a remarkably deep and contradictory fellow. No sooner have I explained to you that I've given up having opinions, strongly implying that it might behoove you to do the same, than I'm confessing the nostalgia I've been feeling lately for people who are able to separate Good from Bad.

Specifically, I'm longing for the firm but gentle voices that were so common in the early days of television, people like Ward Cleaver (played by Hugh Beaumont—an ordained minister, incidentally) and Arlene Francis. Probably I'm more in the market for Arlene, who was a racy theater gal, than for Ward, whose firm but gentle idea of the Good would likely have expunged me. The Good changes through time, often for the better, so I suppose that what I miss in those mellow tones is not a particular set of values but the indefeasible feeling they conveyed that the Good existed and might, with an effort of will, be discerned from the Bad—a belief in wholeness, you might call it.

This longing comes over me most forcefully when I'm exposed to commentary, as I am all the time—as who isn't? Criticism, which used to be a secondary practice, now seems to be a tertiary or quaternary one—responses to responses to responses. The matter under discussion is little more than a springboard. The thing itself—the res—barely exists, for all the serious attention it's paid.

When a highly cerebral music reviewer writes at great length about the strategic canniness of the "artist" at the base of some trashy summer hit, deconstructing the auto-tuned breathiness of his negligible voice and the social coordinates of his manufactured appeal, and seems, in some enjoyably defeated way, to admire this farrago of cynicism, I get a little sad.

Similarly, roundtable interpretations of a presidential candidate's tense shoulders and dog-whistle remarks, and analyses of the base these appeal to, remind me that it's been decades since I read the Constitution and nobody much is adverting me to its tenets or to any other foundational principles. This is an exaggeration, of course. Serious people exist. But they tend to be drowned out by these others whose loudness, speed, shallowness, and ubiquity wear me down and diminish my capacity to go slow and think hard. It's as though at some point it was decided that the world is irreparably broken and all that's left for us is to be connoisseurs of the wreckage.

A lot of very fancy writing has resulted from this. You

could smother under the piles of twisting metaphors, jeweled epigrams, aching ironies—all the scintillating despair.

About a year ago, I read an online essay about a woman who, at the time, was world-famous for being absolutely nothing and monetizing the hell out of it. The author was clearly a recent graduate of an Ivy League college that offered a degree in semiotics. The donnée of the piece, as best I can recall, had something to do with the nothing woman's relationship to cosmetics. According to the author, this was cunning and profound and merited an onslaught of erudition. The essay, which was not very long, referenced Foucault, de Saussure, Adam Smith, Camille Paglia, Daniel J. Boorstin, and Helena Rubinstein, among others. It went on to compare its vacuous subject to Nefertiti, Madonna, Clara Bow, Barbra Streisand, and Madame Defarge, and concluded that, by virtue of giving rise to all this tortuous prose, she had Triumphed and the rest of us must surrender to her hegemony.

I forwarded the piece to my friend Jason. In typically offensive style, he wrote back:

"This is a classic example of overthinking a whore."

That isn't exactly what I'm longing for but it's sort of what I'm longing for.

A Paradox Explained

The reformed Jason is much like the first Jason I knew—he is tumultuous with words, with ideas—much of it is humbug, and some of it is boring, but every now and then a thought will hit.

He said something I liked the other day. I was telling him I found it paradoxical that some of the most ardent social reformists in the public eye had reputations for being privately unbearable.

"You're talking about clinical narcissists," Jason said. "It makes perfect sense if you think about it. The clinical narcissist is the most moral person because he identifies his own interests with the Good. And since other people, laboring under the delusion that they're real, too, don't invariably *serve* his interests, the narcissist's most intimate sense of the world is that it's a place of gross inequities. This makes him a crusader."

I was about to say I thought he might be on to something but he wasn't done.

"Hence," he concluded, "my aversion to social justice."

Ignorance

His new equipoise has allowed Jason to see unsuspected values in his past. This is not to suggest that his father is now showing a good side or his mother a less than saintly one, only that he's looking back from an angled distance and he's seeing things more coolly. I'm not so keen on all his findings.

"You have to admit," he said the other day, "in our parents' houses, the highest value was placed on Ignorance because from Ignorance flowed the *enjoyment* of Ignorance."

When I quoted this to Emma, who grew up in a house like the houses we grew up in and is a highly educated woman, I hoped she would pooh-pooh it.

She looked thoughtful.

"Our parents never would tell us what they were *running* from," she said.

So then I conceded, "It was as if there was some kind of Terrible Secret."

"Yes," she said. "They didn't want us to know something . . . as if they were *sparing* us something."

"In a way, it was as if we were in this very tense Garden of Eden and the Tree of Knowledge had these garish neon leaves but there was no serpent to set things going in the right direction."

"No matter how much I read, I feel as if people from other places have more density," she said.

"Yes! When I got to college, even the dumbest-ass preppy idiot had something *filled in*, do you know?"

"I mean, why wouldn't they even tell us what *made* the sump dangerous?"

"I still feel as though every time I walk into a new room, there's going to be a pop quiz," I said.

"I still feel as if I'm catching up," she said.

"But what *was* the secret? What was the terrible thing that happened to all of them? And why did they think it was a good idea to make us stupid?"

"People think, Oh, it was the Holocaust," she said.

"But it wasn't," I said.

"It was *before* that, somehow," she said.

"Oh God, it was before the destruction of the Second *Temple*," I said.

"I've lived in the city more than twice as long as I've lived anywhere else," she said, "but I still don't think I'm completely a city person."

"I still feel as if I'm catching up," I said.

Meaning

I would be embarrassed if I could remember how old I was when I finally understood what the meaning of "meaning" is.

Before that, characters on television and sometimes even real people would cry out, "My life has no meaning!" and I would be baffled.

In those days, I assumed that the meaning of "meaning" was restricted to the definitions of words in the dictionary.

It *does* embarrass me that I never thought to look up the meaning of "meaning" *in* the dictionary.

The Sump

Two blocks away from my childhood home was something we called a "sump."

I don't remember the name of the block the sump was on, even though I lived in that house eighteen years straight and visited it for a quarter century more. I think, vaguely, that it might have been on one of two blocks that had the same name but for an additional vowel in one of them. But I'm not certain that's so, and even when I lived there, I was never able to remember which street had which name. Nor do I remember what the two names were.

The sump was a depression in a patch of land roughly a quarter acre square. It was set off by a double-height chain-link fence and flanked by split-level houses, identical except for color.

There were two models of split-level in the neighborhood and one model ranch. The split-levels originally cost eleven thousand dollars and the ranches ninety-five hundred and split-level people were always a little smug around ranch people.

What I knew about the sump was that IT WAS VERY DANGEROUS!!!!

One was NOT TO GO NEAR IT!!!

And in truth, it must have been dangerous, because at a time of rampaging development, the pooh-bahs behind this neighborhood let it alone.

Another thing I remember about the sump is that, though it was the first ogre of the neighborhood kids' childhood, and therefore should have been muddled in our minds with the murderous kings of biblical stories and the shape-shifters of fairy tales, we were all pretty blasé about it. It was our local Moloch, devourer of tiny people, and we couldn't care less.

Thirty years after the last time I gave the sump a thought, sinkholes became a sort of fad around the nation. Men, nestled in their beds with the new Grisham, were all of a sudden being swallowed up by the earth.

Oh, *that's* what the sump was, I thought: a sinkhole.

There were problems with this, chief among them that a salient characteristic of sinkholes was contagion. If your property abutted one, you were on red alert.

Yet two eleven-thousand-dollar split-levels had been built on either side of our sinkhole and had endured there, stable, for sixty years.

I wanted to think that this was because back in the early fifties the situation had been thoroughly vetted—that we'd been safe—but I'm more inclined to believe it was all a matter of dumb luck.

After all, Nassau County is a suspicious place, where the incidence of breast cancer far exceeds the national average.

I have a friend who contends that that's because of the aquifers.

Trees

In front of the house where I grew up, on a strip of curbed lawn at the far side of the sidewalk and right by the street, were two sycamore trees, spaced to demarcate the western border of the small area that constituted our property.

By the time they got to me, they were very large trees, with widespread branches, and in leaf, they were magnificent.

In the middle of our lawn stood another tree, I never learned what kind. It was skinny and didn't flower much and though there was no reason to believe it wasn't perfectly healthy—an arborist would have approved—I always thought of it as consumptive.

For most of my life, I believed that sycamores were *trees* and all other trees were *kinds* of tree.

Evergreens and redwoods and birches and oaks had, I thought, an air of imposture about them.

When I was in my forties, it hit me that this wasn't so. Each species was sovereign.

It came as a shock. I didn't know what to do about it.

Dinner

Louise was visiting her family out west so I invited Emma to dinner, then Jason called, at loose ends, and on an impulse I invited him, too. They know each other a bit to talk to and better than that by reputation because I squeal on them to each other. Each has always been disposed to the other and I liked the idea of three people in the apartment with everyone talking at once, making a pleasant hubbub. I served a shrimp thing and a salad and for dessert my grapefruit-parsley sauce that you pour over ice cream and everyone becomes emotional. It's wrong for people our age to feel "like" adults; we *are* adults, aging ones, but none of us entirely believes it—there's something arrested about most of the people I'm close to—so an evening without petulance, without rancor, without childish anxieties, without any emotions that aren't amiable and grateful is a rare evening and one we know to value. Emma and Jason got on like a house ablaze, as the old expression goes, and each was happy for something about the other—Jason for

Emma's wedding and Emma—though of course she didn't say so—for Jason's sanity.

Jason was the newsy one. It seems he's becoming more Jewish. He's half Jewish, on his mother's side (which is the side that counts), and he's thinking of turning into one of those half Jews who are far more serious about it than we full Reform, slacker Jews ever seem to be. Though I was sort of stunned by this I held my tongue—everyone was being so kind and adult, and the apartment was in its party mode. Most nights, I keep the lights off, except for some dim ones in the kitchen and the light given off by the TV. I'm content to stumble about in an ecological semi-darkness when I'm alone. When people are over, I turn on the lamps throughout the apartment, at a clement level, and add candlelight to it. The candles give off that nice fragrance of wax and flame and, this night, I'd even gotten Casablanca lilies, which pitched in their festive expensive scent. The atmosphere was radiant and I wasn't going to subtract from it by being skeptical or snide about Jason's new affirmation of faith, though I confess it worried me a good deal. I had recently given up having opinions and depended on Jason's reflex of negativity to balance me out.

"I never took it seriously, 'religion,'" Jason said—a little haltingly for him—"but then we were trained never to take anything seriously, weren't we? That's what made us such smart-asses—not you, Emma—because nothing ever *meant* anything, really."

I noticed that Emma looked sympathetic.

"And of course, *God* was absurd and *faith* was absurd, and I still *believe* that—but the thing is, I was so stupid, I'd completely neglected Recon*struc*tionist Judaism. They see God as a kind of image or metaphor. They just hack off the supernatural aspect, which makes religion so impossible to embrace, and what's left . . . I don't know . . ."

". . . is nice," Emma said.

"Well, yes. It's . . . human or something—nice, it's nice. And you know, I've been at a point for a while, where there hasn't been much going on, really—"

"I wouldn't say that," I protested; a formality.

"You don't have to. I've said it for you. But you know: there was the *insane* period—does Emma know about—"

I confessed: "She does."

"That's okay—really, I'd be sort of offended if you hadn't bothered to mention it—anyway, there was *that*. Then all that time after. Then some kind of exhaustion and . . . I've been a little tired of myself, honestly."

"We all get that way sometimes," said Emma.

"I mean: my *responses* to everything. Everything has to be *seen through*. Every person is just a receptacle of flaws. And *why*?"

This was a rhetorical question.

"All it is is a *mode*—a mode we can't *free* ourselves from."

He looked off to the side and into a middle distance. His eyebrows were working and his mouth was, too. He was trying to formulate his next thought, and he manipulated his face so that we would wait for it and not interrupt with any thoughts of our own. Then he spoke. "I remember I saw this play about thirty years ago."

"Are we on topic?" I asked.

"We are. Anyway, I don't remember what it was called and I don't know if I'd like it now but at the time I found it very moving. Near the beginning of it, there was this scene where the people are squabbling—it's the morning after a debauched night—it's *that* kind of fight—and there's a knocking on the door. They *keep* fighting and the knocking goes on, until finally, someone opens the door and the Gestapo bursts in!"

"Oh my word!" said Emma.

"Yes—only, it was shocking, not funny, it was e*ffec*tive, do you know? Then I read John Simon's review—he trashed it—but the only thing I can remember about the review is that he said it was ridiculous that the Gestapo would have just politely knocked like that. They would have kicked the door in. And maybe that's true—I suppose the Gestapo didn't spend a lot of time knocking—but I thought, Really? That's your gotcha? The Gestapo knocked, therefore it's a bad play? That's all it takes?"

"Well: John Simon," I sighed, for the thousandth time in my life.

"Except you see, I think that's what I've been doing—I think that's what most of us do. Life *comes* at us—this huge, messy *thing*—and all we say is, 'The Gestapo doesn't knock' and good-bye, life! I mean it's not hard to find the flaws in things, the fissures in things, they're everywhere. Do it enough, it becomes a kind of parlor trick. It doesn't mean you're *impressive*. It doesn't mean you're *smart*."

"No," said Emma, and I was concerned that she was starting to like Jason even more.

"I think the mistake we make is we grade everything *down* from the Perfect when we should be grading *up* from the Nonexistent."

I have a long history with people undergoing epiphanic breakthroughs, and it's been demoralizing when it hasn't been chilling. In her time of fresh crisis, Fredda had an epiphany a day that made everything all right forever until, after a couple of years of this, she killed herself. I've had friends who realized that forty years of crushing anxiety had all been a gluten allergy and friends who decided that all they needed was a child, and it's never ended well. What's more, Jason's epiphany hovered uncomfortably close to arrant sentimentality, and when people are giving themselves to sentimentality, they're evangelical about it, and they urge you to contribute a coordinating emotion. This is something I'm not able to do, and the incapacity is one I don't regret. Casting aside my recent vow of neutrality, I raised an objection.

"Look, some things are *deserving* of criticism—some criticism is the only thing saving us from complete—"

"I'm not saying we should be *morons*," he interrupted. "I don't think we should not *notice* anything. I just think maybe we should be more careful choosing what the outweighing factor is."

I didn't know what to say to this. It wasn't that this was some brand-new Jason. He was more like a long-ago Jason, come back without warning—the one I'd first met, when he was straight out of Juilliard, handsome, with that voice, and being called in to audition for absolutely everything, and coming *thisclose* every time. (He was always losing out to Alec Baldwin.) He had a shining sense of destiny then (incorrect, as it turned out) that made him both a blowhard and impossibly likable.

"It's just," he continued, "that I've sort of dismissed people from my life, haven't I?"

"Yes," I said.

"I mean, there's been *zero*."

Jason sometimes dates men and sometimes dates women but for a long time he's dated no one. And most of his friends have peeled off.

Then he said something that seemed to intuit my misgivings.

"And I'm always so afraid of being sentimental— and what a stupid thing to run from! I mean, not real sentimentality—the kind that's a branch of cruelty, that annihilates—but this business of suspecting every feeling of being a con job. Even David Foster Wallace said the really courageous writer would be the one who risked being thought sentimental."

I did not say "for all the good it did him" because (1) shallow jokes about suicides are not funny, and (2) it would have been exactly the sort of remark Jason was inveighing against and I didn't relish the prospect of being turned into Exhibit A.

"Really," he went on, "I think what it is is that I'm becoming attracted to ethics. And you can't have ethics without *people*, so . . ."—and here he lowered his majestic voice to a comic basso profundo—"I'm thinking of enduring people again."

"That's a very good idea," said Emma and lifted her wineglass in a toast.

"For those who are able," I said and, under social pressure, lifted my glass, too.

Jason was about to say something, then decided to say something else instead. He looked at me directly and knitted his brow because what he wanted to say was not easy for him to say or for me to hear.

"You know, under all this . . . *this* . . . there really are a couple of *relatively* nice guys."

"That's *true*," said Emma, her eyes aglow.

And it had been such a pleasant evening before they lost their minds.

Local Character, Part 2

Eight years ago, I was congratulated for not wearing a certain coat.

The coat in question is a beauty: of boiled wool, voluminous but elegant in silhouette, it is most striking for its color, a gorgeous shade of hunter green or olive green or a mix of the two. I'm sure the coat possesses details—extremely subtle details, perceptible to dolphins—that made it on trend when it was new (though they didn't have that phrase then), but it's so exquisitely tailored that I believe it's gone from stylish to classic without ever making a pit stop at dated.

When I first got it, I wore it all the time. I loved it so much that I extended my personal winter so that I could keep wearing it in inappropriate weather, and once I was in it, I wouldn't take it off—not in theaters, not in restaurants, not in office buildings. Not in small, low-ceilinged rooms thick with people. I perspired in it and just drew the lapels in tighter.

I have many other coats. My closet is stiff with them and I was wearing one the day I was congratulated. They're fine, I guess, in their way, but they don't have the power to command my loyalty the way the green coat does, and the person who congratulated me—it was the woman who painted my apartment—did so not because the coat I was wearing was so attractive, she just enjoys variation for its own sake.

The coat had been a gift I received at a photo shoot. I'm as surprised by that as you are. Ordinarily, I would avoid photo shoots like hives—I avoid them even more than they ignore me—but at the time, I had a play on Broadway that was—I'll simply say this—a *hit*, and Fred Weller, an actor who was in it, had been asked to pose with me for a magazine feature on Broadway collaborations. I'm very fond of Fred—this was the third of my plays he'd done and in two of them he'd been naked so I didn't know how to refuse. I thought of the shoot as a kind of war reparation.

The periodical doing this article was a new one called *Show People*.

Show People aimed to be a glossy *Vanity Fair*-style magazine focused on the Broadway theater—this at a time when magazines had given way to zines and the theater had long been recognized to be a minority interest. The first issue was out. Its cover photo was of the movie actress Hillary Swank in costume for her Broadway debut role, a production that by the time the magazine hit the stands had already closed out of town, and the other articles all had titles like "Those Randy Redgraves." The future didn't look bright for *Show People* but they'd committed to a second issue.

We gathered in a room downtown and it was pretty much how you'd imagine. There were assistants all over the place—the types who in most American localities would have been outliers and here represented the *ne plus ultra*—and they were scurrying around at busy cross-purposes and proclaiming the tasks they were being asked to fulfill "*absolute*ly im*pos*sible" twenty seconds before completing them. The show that was being photographed before ours was this very sleek Broadwayed-up production of *La Bohème*, which had several casts, and the room was littered with all these Mimis and Rodolfos who were incredibly good-looking and sort of sweet and always seemed to be falling into poses even when there wasn't a photographer or a mirror or a stylist anywhere to be found. Their every gesture seemed to say, "Opera, yes, but I go to the gym," and I don't know why but I found them charming. I was lost as could be when I slunk into the room—Fred either hadn't arrived yet or had already been led into a primping parlor—and I wedged myself furtively into a corner and looked apologetic. After a few minutes, I was rescued by the magazine's editor. I don't remember her name though I'm sure by now she's a titan. Success radiated from her like quills from a porcupine, and she was gorgeous. She looked exactly like Heather Locklear. I try not to be sloppy about language, so when I tell you she looked exactly like Heather Locklear, what I mean is that had Heather Locklear wandered into the room and found herself at a short distance from the editor, she would have started fussing with her hair, assuming a mirror. *That's* how much she looked exactly like Heather Locklear. She introduced herself to me and couldn't have been nicer, though when, to break the ice, I pointed out that the cover of the inaugural edition of her magazine featured a picture of an already defunct production, she didn't seem to find it all that insightful. To make up, I mentioned that she looked exactly like Heather Locklear. She said that although she'd heard this before, she was really just a Jewish girl from Westchester County. It would have been just like me at that moment to say, "*Obviously* you were adopted," but I was cut off by Baz Luhrmann.

By then, the Mimis and Rodolfos had finished and were making a slow, chaotic, regretful exodus from the room just as a group of Def Poetry Jammers started trickling jauntily in. Meanwhile, Fred showed up. I don't know if he'd been styled or not, but he looked great, as he always does, and we were introduced to the photographer, who is a major player in the story of the green coat.

I wish I could remember these people's names, especially when they're as nice as the photographer was. He was tall and slightly stooped with dark curly hair and, if I remember correctly, some kind of facial hair, not trendy, not a soul patch or anything like that. If you didn't know he was your incredibly chic photographer, you would have taken him for a social studies teacher.

Photographers have a way of being slow and ruminative even when the activity around them is cyclonic, as it was now, with a lot of style attention being given to the jammers. The photographer looked me up and down for a long time. He seemed to empathize with my problem. Something was wrong with my outfit. There was a stylist there, too, who as the photographer was looking me up and down, looked me down and up in rough syncopation. The stylist was the kind of flamboyant homosexual that when you write homosexuals like that homosexuals write to tell you there are no homosexuals like that then other homosexuals write to accuse the first homosexuals of being homophobic. A few years later he would be a judge on *America's Next Top Model*. At a certain point in the session, he murmured that he found me "adorable." I really don't know how they let him be a judge on *America's Next Top Model*.

The kindly photographer, who had begun to refer to my look as my "plight," told me he'd figured out what I was doing—I was trying to hide!—and that I wasn't doing it well enough.

"You know," he said, "on the way over I saw a coat in a store window that might work," and he left.

You would think that in these photo shoots there'd be

all sorts of exigencies of time and money, yet apparently key players can wander off at will to purchase coats.

Truthfully, nothing seemed to come to a halt. The jammers were busily becoming even more hip, and some actors from *Hairspray* started bouncing bouncing bouncing in. Then the photographer returned with my coat. It was as if no time at all had passed.

Love can do that to a guy.

I put it on slowly and stroked it. It was like those scenes they used to have in movies where lower-income women for the first time in their lives would don a full-length mink, back before doing that was just a prelude to getting splashed with paint by PETA members.

"Yes," I think I said but who knows what I said?

Fred seemed to like it, too, as did the stylist, and the photographer looked to my eyes even more lactal with the milk of human kindness than he had before.

The shoot went pretty well—my coat was a shield, it could reverse lightning bolts—and when we were done, I asked to buy it.

The photographer wouldn't let me. He *gave* it to me. In return, all he wanted were some tickets to my show.

So you see the coat is not only a beloved garment but the memento of a greatly generous act.

I don't know what I was thinking the day I was congratulated for wearing something else. Probably the green coat was at the dry cleaner's. That's the only reason I ever substitute for it now.

We're in it for the long haul, I think. A couple of years ago I had a vision and I know it was a true one.

When I am very old, I am going to become a walker. I am going to walk up and down the few streets of my neighborhood, taking everything in, and I will be wearing my green coat. Even in early spring, I will be wearing the green coat. It will be patched in places and threadbare in others. Already, my friend Linda has had to sew back on a button that fell off from sheer fatigue. I don't discount the possibility that one day the buttons won't all match. Some of them may not be flush with their buttonholes. This is fine by me. I will walk in my tattered garment, surveilling my immediate surroundings with a captious eye. People will start to notice me. I will become something of a local character.

I can picture a young man and an older man looking at me.

The young man will nudge the older man and, mistaking me for a homeless person, say, "See that guy? All he ever does is walk around in that green coat."

And the older man, blessed with an encyclopedic knowledge of trivia, will reply, "That 'guy' used to be a regular on Broadway."

"Oooohh," the younger man will say.

Then, puzzled, he'll ask, "What's 'Broadway'?"

Indulgently, the older man will explain: "It's a place where they used to do plays."

"Ooohh," the younger man will say then. "What's 'plays'?"

They will think that I'm senile and that my walking is compulsive or blind. But it won't be and I won't care that they think it is. I will have met my destiny, which is to be a flaneur, a walker in the city, as I would be already, were it not for my tendency to self-quarantine. I will not be oblivious to my environment, I will be rapt with it. I'll be taking in the old buildings that are at present new buildings and the new buildings that will have displaced the old buildings and I will be marveling at how much it's all changed.

The critic Ruskin, before he went mad, wrote that decay is the condition of the picturesque. We will, I think, be wonderfully picturesque, the neighborhood and I.

Who knows? By then even the new Times Square might be something to treasure.

Acknowledgments

I am always made uncomfortable by acknowledgments. They read to me like acceptance speeches for awards that haven't been conferred.

That said, here are mine:

George Lane has been my agent since before either of us was born and is exceptionally good at telling me what I can do with myself. He ordered me to write this book. Paradoxically, he bears no blame for anything in it that's blameworthy.

My newest agent, Simon Green, has been a dogged and very kind advocate. As George told me *to* write this book, Simon explained to me *how* to write this book. I'm grateful.

Sarah Hochman, as editor of a newbie, has been forced to render instruction along the lines of "This is a book. A book has pages. On the pages are words." She has done this, and much more, with clarity and wisdom, and, as of this writing, has not yelled at me once.

Angela Bourke, whom I will probably never meet, wrote

the subtly elegiac biography of Maeve Brennan, *Maeve Brennan: Homesick at the New Yorker* (Counterpoint, 2004), from which I've taken all the facts about Maeve I needed.

Many lovely people innocently posed for their portraits, all the while thinking they were just being my friends. I hope they still think that.

About the Author

Richard Greenberg has written two dozen plays, including the Tony Award–winning *Take Me Out*, which was a Pulitzer Prize finalist, as was his play *Three Days of Rain*. He is the winner of *Newsday*'s George Oppenheimer Award for Best New Playwright and the PEN/Laura Pels Award for a playwright in mid-career. He lives in New York City.